Learning about Language

George Keith

Hodder & Stoughton

A MEMBER OF THE HODDER HEADLINE GROUP

Acknowledgements

The author and publishers would like to thank the following:

Copyright Text:
p1, *Hodder Geography: Rivers and Coasts* © Andrew John (Hodder & Stoughton, 1998); pp7–8, *My Brother Jack* by George Johnston, first published in 1964 by William Collins; pp15–16, *In Search of History – 1066-1485* © J. F. Aylett (Hodder & Stoughton, 1983); pp23–24, *The Dinosaur's Investigator's Handbook* © Marc Gascoigne (Puffin Books, 1997); pp31–32, *Exploring the Bismark* © Robert D Ballard (Madison Press, Toronto); pp43–44, *The Next 500 Years* © Adrian Berry (Headline, 1995); pp49–50, *Solos 3* © John Goodwin & Bill Taylor (Hodder & Stoughton, 1996); p59, 'Mowlam to quit . . .' by Andrew Grice, from *The Independent*, 5 September 2000; p60, 'Driven Out . . .' from *The Mirror*, 5 September 2000; p61, 'Voice of the Mirror' from *The Mirror*, 5 September 2000; pp67–72, *Playing Beatie Bow* © Ruth Park (Penguin Books Australia Ltd); p79, *Look No Hands*, © U. A. Fanthorpe, reproduced by kind permission of U. A. Fanthorpe; p79, *The Artist's Room*, © Gillian Clarke, reproduced by kind permission of Gillian Clarke; p79, *Time, Gentle Men*, © Peter Benton, reproduced by kind permission of Peter Benton; p79, *Child With Dove*, © Gregory Harrison, reproduced by kind permission of Gregory Harrison; p92, 'This wasn't swept up . . .' from *The Mirror*, 2 September 2000; p97, 'Final 77 seconds . . .' by Jon Henley, from *The Guardian*, 1 September 2000; p99, BBC Online material (12 September 2000, www.bbc.co.uk/reallywild) reproduced by permission of the BBC; pp105–107, *Pigling and her Proud Sister*, from 'Classic Folk Tales from Around the World' ed. Robert Nye (Leopard, 1996, a division of Random House); pp119, *Finest Hour* © Tim Clayton & Phil Craig, reproduced by permission of Hodder & Stoughton Limited; pp122–123, *Video Nasty*. An episode of 'Only Fools and Horses' by John Sullivan (BBC Worldwide Ltd, 1999); p123, *The Psychology of Language and Communication* © Andrew Ellis and Geoffrey Beattie (Psychology Press, 1986); p124, Advert reproduced from Kirklees Metropolitan Council publication; p126, *Do Angels Wear Brassieres* from 'Summer Lightning' by Olive Senior (Longman, 1986).

Copyright Photos/Illustrations:
p15 Murder of St Thomas a Becket © The British Library;
p35 The launch of the Bismarck Feb 1939 © Bettmann/Corbis;
p64 Mo Mowlam photo from *The Independent* © The Independent/Syndication;
p77 Fleet Street, London 1890s © Corbis; Fleet Street 1980 © www.britainonview.com;
p80 *A Corner of the Artist's Room*, Paris, by Gwen John (1876–1939), Sheffield City Art Galleries;
p80 *Child With Dove*, 1901, Pablo Picasso, National Gallery/DACS;
p80 *Lala at the Cirque Fernando*, 1879, by Edgar Degas, National Gallery;
p80 *Golconde*, 1953, by Rene Magritte (1898–1967), The Bridgeman Art Library/Lauros-Giraudon;
p117 Dick Tracy cartoon strip, from *Dick Tracy: America's Most Famous Detective*. Edited by Bill Crouch Jr, Plexus Publishing Limited © 1987 Tribune Media Services;
p118 Martin Luther King © Bettman/Corbis;
p124 1930s advertisements, from *Ragtime to Wartime: The Best of Good Housekeeping 1922-1939* published by Ebury Press © 1986 by The National Magazine Company Limited. Reprinted by kind permission of Hoover and Glaxo Smithkline.

Every effort has been made to trace copyright holders of material reproduced in this book. Any rights not acknowledged here will be acknowledged in subsequent printings if notice is given to the publisher.

Orders: please contact Bookpoint Ltd, 130 Milton Park, Abingdon, Oxon OX14 4SB. Telephone: (44) 01235 827720, Fax: (44) 01235 400454. Lines are open from 9.00 am–6.00 pm, Monday to Saturday, with a 24 hour message answering service. Email address: orders@bookpoint.co.uk

British Library Cataloguing in Publication Data
A catalogue record for this title is available from The British Library

ISBN 0 340 78000 2

First published 2001
Impression number   10 9 8 7 6 5 4 3 2 1
Year   2005 2004 2003 2002 2001

Copyright © 2001 George Keith

Cover image by Mike Stones.
Typeset by Fakenham Photosetting Ltd, Fakenham, Norfolk, NR21 8NN.
Printed in Great Britain for Hodder & Stoughton Educational, a division of Hodder Headline Plc, 338 Euston Road, London NW1 3BH by J.W Arrowsmiths, Bristol.

Contents

INTRODUCTION

In this book you are going to study the English language and its uses, especially in reading and writing. Some of you may be fortunate enough to know one or more other languages as well as English.

Whichever language or languages you know, you learned language by using it because you needed it: by listening and talking to others and by reading and writing.

Language study means thinking about language, thinking about how you and other people use it. To do this you need to look at words and their meanings, at spellings, at grammar and punctuation, and at different kinds of texts.

Each unit in this book will give you a text to read and will ask you to write a text of your own. Sometimes there will be more than one text to read.

A text is a sequence of words and sentences doing a particular job. It could be a letter, a story, a newspaper article, a homework essay or an e-mail message. The word comes from the Latin 'texere' meaning 'to weave', so it means language woven together to do a job. You probably know two related words, 'textile' and 'texture' which have similar meanings.

Between the reading and the writing you will look at words, spellings, grammar, punctuation and how texts are put together. Language study is like doing a jigsaw: gradually the bits join up to make the whole picture. At the back of the book there is a glossary (a short dictionary) to help you check the meaning of anything you are not sure about.

UNIT ONE: *The Hydrological Cycle*

TEXT: FROM *RIVERS AND COASTS* BY ANDREW JOHN (HODDER & STOUGHTON EDUCATIONAL, 1998)

Reading

Read the following text on the Water Cycle. Make sure you read it twice. If some of the long words seem difficult, look at them closely and say them to yourself slowly.

What Is The Hydrological (Water) Cycle?

The circulation of water from the oceans to the atmosphere, to the land and back to the oceans is called the Water Cycle or HYDROLOGICAL cycle. Hydrology is the study of water. The cycle involves several processes. When the ocean is warmed up by the sun, some evaporation may occur resulting in water changing from the liquid into a vapour. Air containing the water vapour rises from the earth's surface, expands and is cooled into drops of water. This is called condensation. The water falls to earth in either liquid or solid form as precipitation (the collective word for rain, sleet, snow and hail). It is then stored as ice (in glaciers), water (in lakes and in the soil) or returned to the oceans and seas. Most water returns to the sea through rivers as surface run-off. The rest returns as groundwater through the soil and rocks.

Summary

Write in one sentence (two if you really have to, but try for one) what the text is about.

Begin with something like, 'The Water Cycle . . .'

Discussion

1 Once you get used to them, the long words in science are not so difficult after all. They are mainly the names of things. Why do you think it is important that science uses specialised names?

2 When you watch a weather forecast on TV, how many of the symbols on the weather chart are directly about the hydrological cycle?

3 Lots of things in life are said to be cyclic, e.g. the life cycle of a tadpole. Think of other things in life that are cyclic.

Words and Spellings

1 There are some long, technical words that you couldn't help but notice in the text. The text is written in English yet surprisingly, many of the words are not English in origin. Look at the word 'Hydrology'. It comes from two Ancient Greek words, 'hydros' meaning water and 'ology' meaning the study of a particular subject, in this case the study of water. Notice that the 'os' has been dropped in the English spelling. English uses lots of words beginning with 'hydro'. How many words can you think of beginning with this prefix? When you have thought of all the 'hydro' words you can, look in a dictionary and see if you can find any more.

2 Find the following words beginning with 'hydro' that mean:

- a speedboat
- a certain kind of bomb
- an acid
- a gas
- a type of pump or brake
- a disease that causes fear of water.

3 Sometimes the 'hydr' bit comes in the middle of a word, for example 'dehydrated'. Find out what 'dehydrated' means. It may have happened to you on a hot summer day or when you were ill once.

4 The 'hydro' words are quite a big family; so too are the 'ologies'. Write down as many words as you can that end with the suffix 'ology'. They are not so easy to find in a dictionary because suffixes come at the ends of words. Some dictionaries list suffixes along with words, so look under 'o' just in case. It may give you some examples.

5 Find out which 'ology' words mean the following:

- the study of life forms
- the study of the earth's crust
- the study of animals
- the study of weather (and what have 'meteors' got to do with it!?).

6 There are other words in this text that come from Latin, another language of the Ancient World. You will often find that Latin words come from Greek but the great difference between the two alphabets makes them seem like different words. Look at 'condensation' and 'evaporation'. Both belong to a big family, for example:

condensation → condense (notice the silent 'e' at the end of condense) and
evaporation → vapour (note what happens to the 'u').
Find all the other members of these two families.

7 Find one or two words that belong to the 'precipitation' family. These will have tricky spellings and are not the easiest of words to pronounce.

8 'Pre' is another prefix, a Latin one this time. Even the word 'prefix' has a prefix in front of it! It means 'fixed in front'. Think of as many words as you can that begin with 'pre' and then check in the dictionary to find some more. Write a list of seven altogether and learn their meanings and their spellings.

9 Alongside Greek and Latin technical terms there are also a number of words that originated as English words, for example 'water', 'rain' and 'hail'. Using a dictionary, check which language the following words come from:

- ocean
- sleet
- atmosphere
- snow
- cycle
- drops
- liquid.

For the next exercise you will need a dictionary with etymologies. Etymology is another 'ology', this time the study of where and how words originate. Etymologies are given at the end of a dictionary entry. Here is an example: the word 'collective'.

Decide what the shortest form of the word is. In this case it is 'collect'. Look up the word 'collect'. Read through the definitions and examples. At the end you will find information about the origin of the word:

[from L collectus = to gather]

L is a code for Latin. Other code signs are:

- Gk = Greek
- OE = Old English (up to 1150 AD)
- ME = Middle English (1150 to 1400)
- MF = Middle French (1300 to 1600)
- OHG = Old High German (up to 1100).

Grammar and Punctuation

1 Nearly all the sentences you write will be statements, questions or commands.

- When you use a **command**, you *tell* somebody *to do* something, e.g. Give me my pen please.
- When you use a **question**, you *ask* somebody something, e.g. Who's got my pen?
- When you use a **statement**, you *tell* somebody something, e.g. This is my pen.

Which one of these is used as the title of the text on page 1?
What kind of sentence are all the others in the text?

2 There are a lot of 'things' in this text, e.g. water, oceans, atmosphere, land, the water cycle, study, processes. Some are singular, others plural. Many are introduced by the word 'the' or 'a'.

> 'The' is called the **definite article** because you definitely know which 'thing' it refers to. 'A' ('an' before words beginning with a vowel) is called the **indefinite article** because you cannot be sure which particular 'thing' it refers to.
>
> 'Thing' is a handy word, but a technical word used in grammar is NOUN which covers words used to name a person, place or thing. The names of persons (your own name, for example) and places (where you live or the name of your school) are called **proper nouns** and are usually written with a capital letter at the beginning. Advertisements and e-mails often don't use capital letters. The rest are called **common nouns** and do *not* have a capital letter at the beginning.

Look through the text and find ten nouns. A good clue to many of them will be the use of an article in front. Count how many times the definite article is used in this text. You should not be surprised to learn that this is the word most frequently used in both spoken and written English. Why do you think it is so popular? What would be the problem in English if it didn't exist? Look back at some pieces of writing you have done at school (any subject) and see how often you have started a sentence with the word 'the'.

3 If you didn't already know, you may have noticed that sentences in writing begin with capital letters and end with full stops. There can be no argument about how many sentences there are in this text – ten. All you have to do is count the full stops. They are easy things to forget when you are busy getting your ideas down on paper, but always remember to check them when you have finished.

If capital letters and full stops are the front and back doors of a sentence, there is also another punctuation mark that is sometimes used inside sentences. It is called a **comma**.

Look for sentences in this text that contain at least one comma, and copy them out. Write the sentences underneath each other.

4 You should have written out four sentences. Are they longer than the ones without commas? Why?

5 Read each sentence aloud (not too quickly), pausing a little at the commas. You need only look at commas on the line, not at the one above the line in 'earth's' which is an apostrophe. (There'll be more about apostrophes in a later unit). Why do you think the commas are there? Find commas that are separating a list of nouns and others that split the sentence into different parts. Read the sentences aloud again to check.

Now write a sentence about commas beginning, 'Commas are used for . . .'

6   Look for other punctuation marks. You should find three different ones. Notice the question mark at the end of the sentence indicating that it is a question sentence.

7   Brackets are also used. What do you think they are used for? Why have brackets been used round 'water' in the title and round 'in glaciers' later on in the text? You may also have noticed a hyphen in 'run-off'. There will be more about this in a later unit when you'll look at how English words are put together.

8   Write down three sentences of your own that contain a special word that needs explaining, for example:

> This is the apex (the top) of the triangle.
>
> There was an equestrian statue (somebody on a horse) in the market place.
>
> Move the cursor (the flashing little black bit) to the top of the screen.

 # Your own writing

1   The main purpose of this text is to explain something in geography, using scientific information. It is written for people about your age. Notice how the text asks a question in the title and then answers the question in the paragraph that follows. This is a tidy way of doing the job. You could also explain the Water Cycle by drawing a diagram with labels. Have a go at doing this, using the information provided in the text.

2   Think of something you could explain to a reader in a paragraph of the same length. Think first of a hobby or interest that you have and then choose a topic. Write your title in the form of a question, for example: How do homing pigeons know the way home? or How does a CD work? Make sure you begin at the beginning, explain any special words and write as clearly as possible.

UNIT TWO: *Mischief*

TEXT: FROM CHAPTER ONE OF *MY BROTHER JACK* BY GEORGE JOHNSTON (FONTANA/COLLINS, AUSTRALIA, 1964)

 # Reading

The text below comes from a novel by an Australian writer, George Johnston. The story is told through Davey, whose parents are away on war service. Davey has an elder brother, Jack, and an elder sister, Jean. There is also a two-year-old sister, Marjorie. All of them are being looked after by Granny.

Read the text and summarise it in four sentences.

On Jack, the effect of the absence of both our parents at the war had been to make him wild and adventurous and reckless. He was fighting other kids in the streets, and usually winning. More and more often he would go truant from school—we used to call it "playing the wag"—especially when he learnt to forge Mum's and Dad's signatures impeccably and could write his own excuse letters to his teachers ... there had even been some minor scrapes with the police. He gave poor old Granny, our seventy-year-old guardian, a terrible time from the very beginning. He regarded me, tolerantly enough but without any mincing of words, as a "bloody sawny little sonk," and it is perfectly true that the period which had turned him into a wild one had made me something of a namby-pamby. Jean bullied me, Jack despised me, my younger sister was a nuisance and a tell-tale, so I clung to my grandmother then as I did later, when the troopship came home. The mischief with which I involved her was always unintentional. Like the terrible day of the Dollicus seeds.

What sort of creeper the Dollicus really was is something of which I have no idea to this day, but that was what it was always called. (Granny had a rare malapropism with botanical names: the rhododendron was the "rota," our pelargoniums became the "paragonia," the hydrangea was always the "hyter." Still, for all I know she might have been pedantically right for once with this creeper, because botanical names often derive from Ancient Greek and *dolikos* is a perfectly good Greek word meaning "long" and this particular creeper was certainly a fantastically long one and the seeds it bore were carried in long thin black pods.) It was ink-dark, huge, dank, and insect-haunted and although it often scared the wits out of me at night it was useful on rainy days because it carried thousands of hard pellet-like little seeds in its pods—in a Daisy air rifle you could use the seeds in place of BB shot—some of them white and some of them black, and these I would collect and arrange on the linoleum-covered floor in a complicated make-believe game which was supposed to represent battles between the Germans and the Aussies.

continued

I was doing this one rainy morning when my grandmother came home from shopping, by which time my private Armageddon had spread from the sleep-out to the vestibule. Granny opened the back door, shook her umbrella, and stepped inside. The combination of her wet shoes, the waxed linoleum, and the scattered Dollicus seeds was too much: her feet slid from under her, and down she came with a crash which, considering how frail and tiny she was, sounded quite awful. But worse than this, her shopping basket went high in the air, then followed her down, a bag of new-laid eggs falling and breaking in a paste of yolk and albumen exactly on the grey crown of her aged head. The shock of witnessing and being responsible for this grotesque disaster plunged me into immediate panic. I fled through the back door, scaled the wall of the outdoor privy, from there scrambled to the roof of the house, clawed my way up the slippery gable to the brick chimney, and sat myself shivering on top of it.

I stayed up there for two hours, with Granny raging around the garden below me, threatening me with a brandished tablespoon and a bottle of castor-oil. Eventually it was my fear of the height that proved too much for me, and I was cold and wet and desperately unhappy and I had to come down.

To my amazed relief she didn't punish me at all, and when she put her arms around me very tightly and kissed me I realised she was crying.

Discussion

Make sure you have first written a summary of the text.

1 The text is about three main topics. What are they? Where does each begin?

2 In what ways are the two brothers different from each other?

3 When you were younger, did you ever have a disaster in your life like 'the terrible day of the Dollicus seeds'?

Words and Spelling

1 The text in this unit is quite a bit longer than the text in Unit One yet it is easier to read, except possibly for the section on the names of plants. Why do you think it is easier to read?

2 There are all kinds of words and phrases in this text: everyday English, everyday Australian English, Greek, and words from Latin.
Find three of each of the following:

● Australian words or phrases
● English words from Latin (they tend to be long ones, like 'impeccably')
● Greek names

Check the ones you think come from Latin or Greek in a dictionary, just to be sure.

3 Check the meanings of 'impeccably', 'Armageddon', 'vestibule', 'grotesque', 'brandished'. Write each one in a sentence of your own that shows the meaning of the word.

4

> 'Malapropism' is a made-up word. It comes from the name of a comic character (Mrs Malaprop) in a play (*The Rivals*) by Sheridan. (Find out later who Richard Brindsley Sheridan was). The name is made up of the French words 'mal à propos' meaning 'out of place' or 'unsuitable'. Poor Mrs Malaprop was fond of using long words but often got them wrong. For example, she describes somebody as 'the very pineapple of politeness' when she really means 'pinnacle of politeness'. On another occasion she says 'Oh! It gives me the hydrostatics' when she really means 'hysterics'. (You should be able to work out incidentally, what 'hydrostatics' means if you have already done Unit One).

It is easy to make fun of malapropisms. Sometimes they are silly, but sometimes they are slips of the tongue. We can all make those, so beware! Some slips of the tongue happen quite often. They are usually words that have similar beginnings and endings. Look at the following common ones, and write down the word that should have been used:

a) Don't make an expedition of yourself.
b) A musician made a rabbit come out of a hat.
c) She saved him from the poisonous snake bite by injecting him with an anecdote.
d) Words of more than three cylinders can be difficult to pronounce.

The following slips of the tongue are called 'spoonerisms'. What has gone wrong?

> **a)** The cobbler holed and sealed the girl's boots.
> **b)** The genie vanished before she could finish her half-warmed fish.

Find out who Doctor Spooner was.

5 Some everyday phrases are difficult to translate from one variety of English to another, though everyone who uses them knows exactly what they mean, e.g. I was gutted; It does mi' ead in; She's dolally.
Jack calls Davey a 'sawny little sonk'. What on earth could this mean? Davey gives us a clue at the end of the sentence.
What words or phrases would you use to describe 'a sawny little sonk'?
Delboy, in *Only Fools and Horses*, for example, is always calling his brother Rodney, 'a right plonker'. Could that be the same thing as a 'sawny little sonk'?

6 Davey uses the word 'mischief' to describe Granny's accident. Would you call it mischief?

7 Davey uses informal words like 'Granny', 'kids', 'Mum', 'Dad'. Find the examples. He also uses more formal words like 'parents', 'grandmother' and 'guardian'. Find these.

There is a very wide range of formal and informal names for family and friends, e.g. mother, mam, mummy, ma etc. Write down as many as you can think of for parents, grandparents, brothers, sisters and friends (for example 'mate'). When do you use formal names and informal ones?

8 Notice that the 's' in 'mischief' is not doubled as it is in the word 'witnessing' (fifteen lines from the end). It would be very convenient if we could make a rule that says 'single "s" before a consonant; double "s" before a vowel' as in the following examples:

mischief; mischance; misdeeds; mistake
witnessing; missing; mission; missal

But would it work out? Use your dictionary to find the evidence for 'yes' or 'no'.

9 The English alphabet contains 21 consonants and 5 vowels (a, e, i, o, u). Spoken English however, uses 20 different vowel sounds, which is a major cause of common spelling problems. What also complicates matters is that the five vowels of the alphabet are often used in pairs to cover the 20 vowel sounds we make when speaking English.

> Pairs of vowels, e.g. 'oa', 'ie', 'ai' and 'oo' are called 'vowel digraphs'. You can easily work out the meaning of 'digraph'; 'di' means 'two' or 'twice' and 'graph' means 'written'.

Look through the text and find examples of words that contain a vowel digraph. List the words under the first vowel of the digraph. You will need five headings: a, e, i, o, u.

The first ten examples have been done for you below. The digraphs have been underlined. Add another ten words.

a	e	i	o	u
	str<u>ee</u>ts	espec<u>ia</u>lly	advent<u>u</u>r<u>ou</u>s	us<u>ua</u>lly
	l<u>ea</u>rnt		w<u>ou</u>ld	tr<u>ua</u>nt
	t<u>ea</u>chers		sch<u>oo</u>l	
			c<u>ou</u>ld	

10 You could divide the first ten examples into two groups: vowel digraphs that are pronounced as one sound, and vowel digraphs that are pronounced as two sounds. There are two obvious ones that are pronounced separately and one example which some people pronounce as one sound while others pronounce it as two. Which do you think these words are?

Are there any digraphs in the second ten words, in which the two vowels are pronounced separately?

11 Look for another ten words containing vowel digraphs. You will now be able to do a survey to see which vowel combinations seem most common, fairly common and least common. Make three lists.

Look now at one particular combination: 'ea', which is very common. List all the words you can think of that contain this vowel digraph. Look through other texts in this book to help you. Look through a dictionary as well. Sort the words into three columns: those *beginning* with 'ea'; those *ending* in 'ea'; and those with an 'ea' somewhere in the *middle* of the word.

Which is the longest list?

Now say the words aloud to a partner and find out how many different ways there are of pronouncing the 'ea'. In the sentence: 'I was reading in Reading', for example, there are two pronunciations. The headline, 'Teachers Learn To Create Storms At Weather Centre' contains no less than four pronunciations! There is an 'ea' combination in the word 'hideaway'. What makes it different?

12 In a notebook, begin to collect interesting words with a vowel combination in them. Are there any words with three vowels in a row?

You could concentrate on words with an 'ie' and an 'ei' in them. The 'i' before 'e' except after 'c' rule often works, but look out for words like 'weird', 'eiderdown' and 'neither'.

Words with a 'uu' in them are very rare: vacuum; continuum. Where do they come from? A dictionary will tell you.

13 Are there any examples in this text of words containing the letter 'y' as a vowel?

Grammar and Punctuation

1

> This text is written in the first person. This means it uses the 'I' pronoun, which is called 'the first person singular'. The first person plural is 'we'. A PRONOUN is a word that can be used instead of a NOUN. Instead of saying 'Sarah', 'Edward' and 'bicycle' every time, you can substitute 'she', 'he' and 'it'.

Look through the text and find out how many times the following pronouns are used:

I,   we,   she,   he,   it,   they,   me,   us,   her,   him,   it,   them.

2

> Another way to narrate a story is to use the third person pronoun: he, she or it, instead of repeating a name every time.

What difference do you think it makes for a story to be told in the first person (I was scared and I hid in a large cupboard at the end of the corridor) and in the third person (John was scared and he hid in a large cupboard at the end of the corridor)?

Look at the paragraph beginning, 'I was doing this one rainy morning . . .', and rewrite it in the third person. Begin by changing the 'I' and the 'my' in the first sentence to 'He' and 'his'. Imagine you are writing it from Granny's point of view.

3

> NOUNS are the names of persons, places and things.

Look through the text and find ten nouns. Write them down.

4 Many phrases (groups of two words or more) are made up of nouns and ADJECTIVES. There are a number in this text: excuse letters, minor scrapes, terrible time, botanical names, long thin black pods.
Find five more examples.
In English, adjectives almost always come in front of nouns. If you know some French, you will have noticed how, in that language, they come *after* nouns, as in: vin rouge; pommes frites; Mont Blanc; café noir.
Write three sentences, each beginning with a phrase containing two adjectives and a noun.

5 Find the sentence beginning, 'I was cold and wet . . .'. How many adjectives are there in it, and which are they? Note that adjectives often follow the verbs 'am', 'is', 'was', 'were' and 'are'.

6 There is one kind of writing in which nouns in English are followed by adjectives. An index to a catalogue, for example, may set out its nouns and adjectives in the following way:

Trousers:
- combat
- corduroy
- cotton
- flannel
- leather
- sports
- waterproof
- woollen

Notice the alphabetical order of the adjectives.
Make a list of your own with five or six different varieties of something.
Choose your own topic and remember that each adjective should tell a reader the kind of thing it is, for example

Cars:
- armoured

- family
- racing
- sports
- toy

7 There is no conversation in this text and therefore no direct speech marks (sometimes called 'inverted commas'). But there are some words printed in inverted commas. Find them and list them. Why do you think inverted commas have been used?

8

> Punctuation marks (like the inverted commas, for example) send signals to readers; they tell you something.

Search the text for examples of the following punctuation marks:

- brackets
- triple dots (sometimes used to show something missing or to create a dramatic pause)
- dashes
- hyphens

Why have they been used in this text?

Your own writing

You are going to do two pieces of writing telling the same incident from two different points of view.

First, think of an incident in your life that you remember well. It needs to be something that involved another person – a relative, a friend, a total stranger. Write about it in the *first person*.

Secondly, think about the incident from the other person's point of view. How might that person have looked at you and thought about you? Write the same incident but this time in the *third person*.

Make sure you use some adjectives. Don't go overboard with them, but choose carefully the ones you do use so that the reader will enjoy them.

Before starting to write, look again at George Johnston's text. Notice how he first puts the reader in the picture by giving some family background. Notice too, how the author rounds off the story with Davey and Granny back on good terms again. Make sure you organise your writing in a similar way. You don't have to focus on a brother; your character may be an only-one, but give the reader some idea of context.

Context is the situation or circumstances in which things happen. Johnston's story is set in a family context.

UNIT THREE: *A True Tale of Murder*

TEXT: FROM *IN SEARCH OF HISTORY, 1066–1485* BY J.F. AYLETT, (HODDER & STOUGHTON EDUCATIONAL, 1983)

Reading

The following text was written soon after the murder in 1170 of the Archbishop, Thomas Becket in Canterbury Cathedral. It tells a grim tale, and oddly enough, was written by a man called Edward Grim (no relation to the brothers Grimm, who wrote the famous fairy-tales centuries later). You can see a drawing of Edward Grim in the picture below. He is the one on the right.

The King of England, Henry the second, had made Thomas Archbishop of Canterbury, believing that he would support the King's policies. In fact they disagreed on many things and Henry turned to the Archbishop of York when he wanted someone to crown his son the future King of England. Thomas was furious and excommunicated the Archbishop of York (this means that he expelled him from the Church). At this Henry was furious. Five of his knights decided to take matters into their own hands and rode to Canterbury to murder Thomas.

The language of the original text has been modernised to make it easier to read but nothing else has been changed. Read it and write in a sentence (or two) a summary of exactly what happened.

> In mad fury, the knights called out, 'Where is Thomas Becket, traitor to the King and country?' Without fear, he came down from the steps, where he had been dragged by the monks who were afraid of the knights. In a clear voice he answered, 'I am here. I'm no traitor to the King, just a priest. I am ready to suffer in His name; far be it from me to run away from your swords.' 'Forgive those people you have excommunicated,' they cried.
> He answered, 'I will not.'
> 'Then you shall die,' they cried, 'and get what you deserve.'
> 'I am ready,' he replied, 'to die for my Lord, so the Church can have its freedom. But in the name of Almighty God, I forbid you to hurt any of my people.'
> Then they made a rush at him, pulling and dragging him roughly, trying to get him outside the church to kill him or carry him off as a prisoner.

continued

But when he could not be forced away from the pillar, one of them seized hold of him and clung to him more closely.

The archbishop shook him off, saying, 'Don't touch me. You owe me loyalty. You and your accomplices are acting like madmen.'

Filled with rage, the knight waved his sword over Becket's head. 'I owe you no loyalty,' he cried, 'compared with my loyalty to the King.'

Then the martyr understood that the hour had come that would release him from the miseries of this life. He bent his head and joined his hands together to pray. He had hardly spoken when the wicked knight, afraid that Thomas might be rescued and escape, suddenly leapt upon him and wounded him in the head, cutting the top. With the same blow, he almost cut off my arm.

Then he received a second blow on the head but still stood firm. At the third blow he fell on his knees and elbows, offering himself as a sacrifice. He said in a low voice, 'For the name of Jesus and the protection of the Church, I am ready to die.' Then the third knight inflicted a terrible wound as he lay there. By this stroke, the sword was broken against the pavement. The top was cut off his head so that blood stained the cathedral floor. The fourth knight prevented anyone from interfering. The fifth man put his foot on the neck of the holy priest and scattered his brains and blood over the pavement, calling out, 'Let us away. This fellow will get up no more.'

Discussion

1 List the different people in the story. Write your impressions of two of them.

2 How can you tell that it is an eyewitness account? What are your impressions of the eyewitness?

3 Becket is described as a 'martyr'. What is a martyr? Do you know of any other martyrs? What is martyrdom? Is it heroism or just bad luck – being in the wrong place at the wrong time?

Words and Spelling

1 Quite a few words in this text have something to do with religion. List which ones you think they are, and check the meanings of any you are not sure about.

2 Look through the text and find the words 'church' and 'Church'. Why do you think one doesn't begin with a capital letter, when the other does? Is the 'church' ever called anything else in the text?

Sometimes 'capital letters' are called 'upper case' and 'little letters', 'lower case'. This is a reminder of the days when printers had two boxes for the metal letters of the alphabet. The upper box, or case, contained the alphabet in capitals, the lower case contained the alphabet in 'little letters'.

3 List the words and phrases that tell you Edward Grim was truly a witness to the murder.

4 Pick out the words that tell you Edward Grim supported Thomas and not the knights.

5 Look up the origins of the following words (you will need a dictionary that gives etymologies):

- knight
- king
- monks
- sacrifice
- traitor
- excommunicated
- prisoner
- pavement
- archbishop
- accomplices
- martyr.

Do you think the word 'pavement' might have changed its meaning between 1170 and the present day?

Write down all the words you can think of or find out, that belong to the 'communicate' word family. Be warned, it's a big one! Why do you think it has so many uses?

6 Find a word that 'proves' the spelling rule 'i' before 'e' except after 'c', and one that is an exception to the rule.

Think of other words that do not fit the rule. To start you off, look in the dictionary for any words beginning with 'ei'.

Collect as many examples as you can of words with 'ei' and 'ie' in them (this may need to be an ongoing project for a wall display) and decide for yourself the statistical reliability of the 'i' before 'e' except after 'c' rule. 'Statistical reliability' means the frequency with which 'ei' follows 'c'.

Do you think the fact that the 's' in 'seized' and the 'c' in 'received' sound the same, might have something to do with it?

7 Look through the text and list all the vowel digraphs (remember, a digraph is a pair of vowels). Group them into the different kinds.

Do your findings confirm the possibility of 'ea' being the most frequently occurring digraph?

8 In this text, two silent letters occur quite frequently. Which are they? Remember, silent letters are consonants that are not pronounced, for example, the 'b' in 'debt'.

 # Grammar and Punctuation

> VERBS are words which tell you what happened; what was done in the text. In that sense, verbs are 'doing words', but you have to remember that the two most frequently used verbs are *not* 'doing words'. These are 'to be' (e.g. am, is, was, were, being, been and so on) and 'to have' (e.g. has, had, having, will have and so on). Notice too, that a very obvious 'doing word' like 'run' is often combined with 'being' and 'having' words (e.g. am running, will run, is running, was running, been running, have run, will have run, and so on).

> Sometimes verbs are used as single words, as in 'The cat SAT on the mat' or 'The dog ATE the bone', but often they are a group of words, for example, 'The cat WILL BE SITTING on the mat' or 'The dog WILL HAVE EATEN the bone'.

Look at the series of verbs below. They have been taken from the text as far as '. . . clung to him more closely.' The words in brackets are there to show who did the verb:

> (the knights) called out . . . is . . . (he) came down . . . (he) had been dragged . . . (who) were afraid . . . (he) answered . . . (I) am . . . I'm . . . (I) am . . . to suffer . . . be . . . to run away . . . Forgive . . . (you) have excommunicated . . . (they) cried . . . (He) answered . . . (I) will not . . . (you) shall die . . . (they) cried . . . get . . . (I) am . . . to die . . . (Church) can have . . . (I) forbid . . . to hurt . . . (they) made . . . pulling . . . dragging . . . trying to get . . . to kill . . . carry . . . (he) could not be forced . . . (one) seized hold . . . clung . . .

These are the words where the action is; they tell you what people did. Notice how often though, a form of 'to be' or 'to have' occurs. Count the number of times a form of 'to be' occurs. Don't miss the 'am' in 'I'm'. There are 16 altogether. Do the same for forms of the verb, 'to have'.

There are also some verbs that begin with 'to', for example 'to suffer' and 'to hurt'. These are called INFINITIVES. How many are there altogether?

Now count how many verbs end with an 'ed', and how many end with an 'ing'.

> Verbs that end with an 'ed' are called PAST PARTICIPLES; the ones that end with 'ing' are called PRESENT PARTICIPLES. The endings are the 'parts' that tell you when the action happened.

Look now at the same passage, but this time with the verbs removed:

> In mad fury, the knights . . . 'Where . . . Thomas Becket, traitor to the King and country?'
> Without fear, he . . . from the steps, where . . . by the monks who . . . of the knights. In a clear voice he . . ., 'I . . . no traitor to the King, just a priest. I . . . ready . . . in His name; far . . . it from me . . . from your swords.
> ' . . . these people you . . .,' they . . .
> He . . .,' I . . . not.'
> 'Then you . . .,' they . . ., 'and . . . what you . . .'
> 'I . . . ready,' he . . . '. . . for my Lord, so the Church . . . its freedom. But in the name of Almighty God, I . . . you . . . any of my people.'
> Then they . . . a rush at him, . . . and . . . him roughly, . . . him outside the church . . . him or . . . him off as a prisoner.
> But when he . . ., . . . away from the pillar, one of them . . . of him . . . and . . . to him more closely.

What different things do you learn about the murder from the two passages? What do verbs do that is different from the other words in the complete text?

Now read the rest of the text, from 'The archbishop shook him off . . .' to ' This fellow will get up no more', and write out all the verbs in the same way as above. Remember, it's the verbs you are looking for.

Compare your version with that of a friend. Discuss any differences and decide which one of you is right. Don't worry if you miss some of the verbs or have written down a word that isn't a verb. You are bound to get most of them. Check with your teacher.

Now look at all the verbs in the second part and organise them into lists. Use the following headings:

Present participles; Past participles; Infinitives; Forms of 'to be'; Forms of 'to have'; Others ending in 'ing'.

Notice that past participles can end with 'en' as well as 'ed'.

Did you also notice the words 'might' in 'might be rescued', and 'would' in 'would release'? These belong to a special group of verbs which you will be looking at more closely in Unit Seven.

Verbs tell you what happened, what is happening and what will happen: time past, time present and time future. To put it another way, they are where the action was, is, or is going to be. Some verbs are quite obviously more 'active' than others. These are called 'dynamic' verbs. Here are some examples:

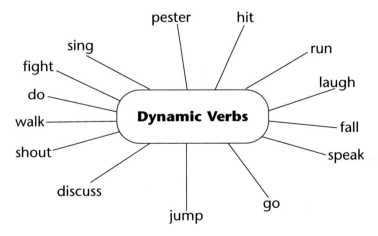

Dynamic verbs refer to action, to something happening. Think of Batman and Robin – the dynamic duo – and you will remember the word and its meaning.

Find some other words in the 'dynamic' word family. Look in a dictionary.

Other verbs are called 'stative'. Sometimes we say, 'He's got himself in a right state', meaning a state of mind.

> Stative verbs refer to states of mind and to feelings, or to a state of affairs.

Some examples of stative verbs are given below:

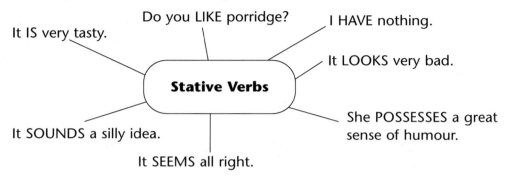

It IS very tasty.

Do you LIKE porridge?

I HAVE nothing.

It LOOKS very bad.

Stative Verbs

She POSSESSES a great sense of humour.

It SOUNDS a silly idea.

It SEEMS all right.

Notice that you have already met two very common stative verbs: 'to be' and 'to have'.

Here is a short piece of writing containing a number of dynamic verbs and one stative verb. How many dynamic ones are there, and which is the stative verb?

> The three of them ran down the steps, jumped into a van, and sped down the road. They were followed by the aliens who looked even more frightening as they began to grow bigger and bigger. Screaming with rage, they stretched out their long tentacles and wrapped them round the van, bringing it to a sudden halt. Jack, Rebecca and Sarah were knocked senseless.

Now here is a piece of writing containing some stative verbs, and three dynamic verbs. Which are they?

> Jack felt sick and his head hurt. It was dark and the van seemed to be lying on its side. Rebecca was a bit dazed and shaken but Sarah was still unconscious. Jack could hear a dreadful screaming sound but he was more angry than scared. The engine was still running, so he pressed hard on the accelerator which scared them off for a little while.

Don't think of verbs as either one or the other: some are dynamic most of the time, others are stative most of the time. Where would you put the following verbs? To sleep; to think; to wonder; to worry; to suppose.

Look again at the account of the murder of Thomas Becket. Are the verbs mostly dynamic or stative?

Your own writing

For this piece of writing you will have to think of a time when you witnessed an event (an accident; a fight; a brilliant goal; a music concert). You can invent something, if you wish, but make sure you write as a witness. Make it interesting for your reader.

Because you are describing what happened, the verbs will be important. Choose them carefully so that a reader will get a vivid idea of what you saw and heard. You do not have to choose a violent event, but you will need to concentrate on the action, as Edward Grim did in his writing. Imagine how difficult it would be for sports reporters, for example, if they didn't have a good selection of verbs to choose from.

Verbs are just as descriptive as adjectives; they help you to see what happened. Use some present participles too, for example: 'The four men, shoving and pulling and groaning, managed to get the piano on to the pavement.'

Notice how the account of Becket's murder is written in short paragraphs. Some consist of one long sentence; others consist of three sentences. What effect do you think this has? Use the same technique in your writing.

It is not surprising that thousands of English adjectives are made from verbs, for example: frying pan; boiled sweets; hiking boots; wishing well; battered fish; fried bread; training kit; cooking pot; fruit-filled pies; a tired-looking lettuce; a worn-out suit; dried tomatoes; spent cartridges; lost property.

Write out the verbs from which these adjectives have come. Use the infinitive, e.g. frying (to fry), boil (to boil).

UNIT FOUR: *Dinosaurs*

TEXT: EXTRACTS TAKEN FROM PP1–2 AND PP117–119 OF *THE DINOSAUR INVESTIGATOR'S HANDBOOK* BY MARC GASCOIGNE (PUFFIN BOOKS, 1997)

 # Reading: Dinosaurs Forever

Aren't dinosaurs brilliant!

Humans love dinosaurs. We're fascinated by these ancient, long-dead creatures. Our culture is full of them. They are the stars of films, television shows and books, and their images are all around us: on t-shirts, toys and posters. Despite their incredibly long, Latin, scientific names, we all manage at a very early age to learn the difference between, say, a Tyrannosaurus rex and a Triceratops.

Some people say it's because they feed into our imaginations. Our fairy stories are full of dragons and other giant beasts – yet here are creatures that once stalked our planet and were easily the equal of any princess-scoffing, overgrown crocodile of legend. Other people say it's simpler than that: we're just fascinated by the very thought that an animal could grow larger than a double-decker bus and stomp around quite happily munching on trees – or sometimes on each other. It's just their very unusual size and appearance that makes us wonder about them so much.

If you stop to think about it for a moment, however, the fascination with dinosaurs is all a bit strange. Look at it this way: have you ever seen a real live dinosaur? Nope, neither have we. All we've ever seen have been reconstructions made by scientists – collections of bones, wired together to make a skeleton, or life-size model built of plaster and resin.

> *But hold on. It is possible to see some dinosaurs that are still alive, and you don't have to go to Jurassic Park.*

Modern dinosaurs

If you want to see a dinosaur right now, go and look out of the window. Go on, try it. See them all? No? 'Course you do! Look at all those little dinosaurs, the ones, with the feathers and the beaks, sitting in the trees and on the fence. Yes . . . birds aren't just related to dinosaurs, they are actually members of the same family of creatures. They really are genuine dinosaurs, albeit without the long necks, the five-tonne bodies or the twenty-centimetre teeth. Somehow, though birds just aren't the same.

Naturalists refer to some creatures as 'living fossils'. This means that they evolved

continued

into their current form a very long time ago – and then stayed in it for millions of years. In effect, they are old-fashioned ... fossils.

Some of these creatures are distinctly mundane. Sharks and rays, with their odd, cartilage-stuffed bodies, are one example. Cockroaches are another; they've outlived the dinosaurs and will probably see us off too, without a single design modification.

The most famous of all living fossils is, of course, the Coelacanth. This odd-looking fish ... was thought to have become extinct in the Cretaceous Period. At least, that is, until December 1938, when a live one was caught by a fisherman off Madagascar. Further specimens have since been caught ... and filmed in water (up to 400 metres down) off the Comoro Islands, north-east of Madagascar.

Living proof?

Could there really be dinosaurs still alive today? The brief answer is simple: a great big no. We have no proof that any have survived, apart from that stuff with the birds, there have been no confirmed discoveries of any dinosaur found anywhere on the planet. Of course, that doesn't stop people reporting a Plesiosaur in Loch Ness, a Diplodocus in the Congo, a Mosasaur off Cornwall, Pterodactyls in Montana, and many more.
However, it is just possible that, given that we have not explored all of the ocean, there could be other ... 'living fossils' like the Coelacanth, hidden down in the depths.

Summarise the text in about three sentences.

Discussion

Make sure you have written your summary before you start this section.

1   What interests you most about dinosaurs? If you are not very interested in dinosaurs, why do you think they have been popular with so many people for so long?

2   Marc Gascoigne is sceptical about recreating a dinosaur from a DNA fragment. On the likelihood of finding a preserved DNA sample, he says: 'Doing all the maths about how likely this all is, then ... well, let's just say you wouldn't want to bet on it. Don't hold your breath.'
Do you think it is worth searching? Why?

3   Were you surprised to learn about the birds and the cockroaches belonging to the dinosaur family? Why do you think they have survived so well? Gascoigne doesn't tell us. Think it through for yourself and then check later with your biology teacher or in an encyclopedia.

Words and Spelling

1 More scientific terminology here for you to look up: find out what the word 'dinosaur' actually means and where it comes from. Is it Greek or Latin?

2 The study of fossils is known as the science of palaeontology, and the people who do it are called palaeontologists. Can you say these words, let alone spell them or know what they mean? Gascoigne got all his information from palaeontologists. Notice the suffix 'ist' which always denotes a person who specialises in whatever the word stands for, for example: botanist, scientist, biologist – and even pessimist and optimist. Can you think of the name for someone who collects postage stamps?
'Palaeontology' is made up of two bits: 'palae-' and '-ontology'. Find out what it means and whether it comes from Greek or Latin. Watch out for the 'ae' when spelling it. The rest is really easy even though it is probably one of the longest words you now know.

3 'Culture' is a funny sort of word, used in all sorts of ways: agriculture, culture-vulture, cultural attaché (whatever is that?), pop culture, a culture on a laboratory dish. The third sentence in this text gives you a good idea of what the author means by the word. Write out the following, 'Among other things, culture is . . . (list the things mentioned in the third sentence). 'Culture' is all sorts of things that lots of people do and like; it's a lifestyle. Again, where does the word come from?

4 Check any of the following words if you are not sure about their meanings: legend, fascination, resin, fossil, evolved, current (not the electrical kind), mundane, cartilage, specimen. Don't just stop at one form of the word, always find a few of its close relatives, for example, evolved/evolution; legend/legendary. Some may not have a big family. Remember when you are doing this, that knowing the meanings of words and using them as soon as you get the chance, is real word power!

5 What do you think is meant by the phrase 'design modification'? Just in passing, here are the word families for these two words:

> Design, designs, designer, designed, designation, designated, designing, sign, signature, signatory, signed, signing, signs, resign, resignation, and so on.
> Modification, modify, modifier, modifiable, modifies, modified, model, mode, and so on.

6 Here are some dinosaur names with their meanings alongside:

> Allosaurus = strange creature
> Archaeopteryx = ancient wing
> Brachiosaurus = arm reptile
> Oviraptor = egg stealer
> Seismosaurus = earthquake reptile
> Velociraptor = speedy predator

Look at the beginning of each technical name and think of one other word similar to it. Look for a clue in their meanings. For example, the 'seismo-' bit has something to do with earthquakes and ah!, I remember, a seismograph is an instrument for detecting and measuring earthquakes. Bingo!

7 Now you are going to investigate the letter 'c' in English spelling. In Old English, 'c' had a hard sound. The 'c' at the beginning of 'cyning' was pronounced like a modern 'k', and is where the word 'king' comes from. After the Norman invasion in 1066, French words, spellings and pronunciations were gradually introduced into the English language. The soft 'c' is just one example of this. The soft 'c' comes at the beginning of such words as 'cell', 'celebrate' and 'celery'.

List all the words in this text that contain a 'c' and work out which is the most frequent, the hard 'c' or the soft 'c'. Make a separate list for words that contain 's' and 'c' together, as in 'fascinated'. How would you describe this? Hard or soft?

Grammar and Punctuation

1 The words writers use (vocabulary) and the way they put them together (grammar) gives a piece of writing its style. How would you describe the style of writing in the dinosaur text?

> **a)** Very formal and stuffy (professor-ish)?
> **b)** Formal, like a school textbook?
> **c)** Informal and chatty?

2 If you thought it was informal and chatty, most people would agree with you. Look at the opening sentence, for example. The text gets off straightaway to a friendly start. It sounds as though the writer is talking to you.

> Another reason for the chattiness is the frequent use of what are called **contractions**. You can always spot them by the apostrophes. The very first word of the text is a contraction: 'Aren't . . .'. The word 'contraction' simply means 'shortened': a bit of a word has been removed and sometimes two words have been joined together. 'Aren't' is really 'are not': the 'are' and the 'not' have been joined together, and the 'o' has been deleted.
>
> Contractions occur very often in speech, where a sound has been omitted. In writing, the apostrophe indicates the missing letter which, in speech, would be a missing sound.

Look through the text and write a list of all the contractions. Then, alongside them, write the complete version, for example:

aren't = are not

In one example, a whole word is missing.

3 In speech, everybody uses contractions; it's a natural part of speaking. In writing, you have to decide when and where to use them. They are used a lot in dialogue, in plays and novels, because dialogue is meant to seem like real talk. In school essays, exam answers and formal letters, most people avoid them; in friendly notes, letters to family and friends and in writing where you want to 'come across' in a more personal way, most people use a few.

If you do use them, you need to watch that apostrophe carefully. Learn the following:

> It's = 'it is' and 'it has'. This is not the same as 'its' *without* an apostrophe, which is a possessive pronoun.

Look at the following examples:

> It's lost its feathers.
> It's a shame its name is such a silly one.
> 'It's a girl,' the midwife cried.
> 'Smack its bottom,' said the doctor.
> 'It's all over,' said the referee.
> Its colour is all wrong.
> It's naughty, but it's nice.

Write seven examples of your own: four 'it's' and three 'its'.

People also sometimes confuse 'where', 'were' and 'we're'.

- 'Where' is about place, and if you remember that its spelling contains 'here', which is also about place, you should sort that one out easily enough.
- 'Were' is the past tense of 'are', nothing more or less.
- 'We're' is a contraction of 'we are'. What could be simpler? Just learn it!

The problem is usually caused by writing what you think you hear. To correct that: stop, look and think which is it?

The same problem happens with 'there', 'their' and 'they're'.

- 'There' is a about a place (it's got a 'here' in it).
- 'Their' is another possessive pronoun.
- 'They're' is like 'we're': it's a contraction of 'they are'.

Finally, the dreaded 'must of', 'would of' and 'could of' which have become very popular in recent years. They may catch on but for the time being it is better to stick to what people have always written.
What you really mean is: 'must HAVE', 'would HAVE' and 'could HAVE'. There's no 'OF' about it. The 'of' is what you are *hearing*; what you are *thinking* is 'have'.

In writing, these words are punctuated like this: 'must've; 'would've'; 'could've'. The written 've' sounds very like 'of' when you say it.

Write out some sentences of your own to show that you know the differences between: 'where, were and we're'; 'there, their and they're'.

Invent a saying that will help you remember for the rest of your life, not to write an 'of' after verbs like 'could, would, may, must, might, should'. If this is a mistake you do not make, invent a saying anyway for the benefit of people who do.

4

> The pronouns 'we', 'us' and 'our' are called **inclusive** pronouns.

Find examples of inclusive pronouns in the text and explain why you think they are called 'inclusive'. Who do they include?

5 You will also find examples of the second person pronoun in this text ('you' and 'your'). Find examples and say why the author has used the second person.

6 Now find a couple of examples of third person pronouns.

7 The author doesn't just use specialist words to do with dinosaurs; he also uses some very ordinary words that are quite difficult to explain but which do very important jobs. Look for:

- despite
- yet
- however
- albeit (that's an odd one)
- though
- in effect.

Don't try to explain them, it's too complicated. Think of a sentence in which you could use one of them. Take some time over it. Don't just put any old sentence; think of an interesting one. Write one sentence for each word.

8 Look again at the opening sentence. It sounds like a question, but is there a question mark at the end? Why do you think there is an exclamation mark? Is it a real question? Discuss this with a partner, and think of some other things people say which seem to be questions but they don't really expect you to answer, for example: 'Isn't it nice weather today!' The answer expected is built into the question.

> People sometimes say things like: 'Do you think I'm stupid or something? Don't answer that!' Questions of this kind are called **rhetorical questions** because they are asked for effect – no answer is required, unlike most questions at school or from parents, which have to be answered, or else!

Think of three rhetorical questions and write them down, for example: Would I lie to you?!

9 How many paragraphs are there in this text? Take note that the first paragraph is only one short sentence long. Writers don't often write paragraphs this short. Why do you think the author did it on this occasion?

10 Notice how the third paragraph is tidily split into two parts by: 'Some people say . . .' And later, 'Other people say . . .'. This is a very useful way of doing things. It's what people mean by a 'structure' in writing. Write a paragraph of your own in which, 'Some people say . . .' and 'Other people say . . .' are included. You will need to think of two different opinions on something, for example: fox hunting; vegetarianism; a pop star.

11 Notice in paragraph seven (about cockroaches), there is a semi-colon followed by the word 'they'. Semi-colons are often followed by words like 'they', 'it', 'you', 'this', 'he', 'they' (pronouns). You could use a full stop if you wished BUT NEVER USE A COMMA! The idea behind using a semi-colon rather than a full stop is to keep the two bits of the sentence together, to make what you say flow better. A full stop separates them too much. Here are some examples:

> Enjoy your holiday while you can; it won't last for ever.
> Give blood; you may need some one day.
> He took my bike without asking; this was the last straw.

Now you write a couple of your own sentences like this.

Your own writing

Marc Gascoigne could not have written his book on dinosaurs so enjoyably, if he hadn't known what he was talking about. To make sure you know what you are talking about, the writing task in this unit comes with lots of information.

Your topic is the beginnings of the Olympic Games in Ancient Greece. On the next page are the bare facts; your task is to rewrite them in a lively and interesting way, as Gascoigne does for dinosaurs. They are not in any particular order. You will need to put them in an order you think best. Don't just copy them out. You will also need to write an opening sentence or two. How about:

Everybody likes watching the Olympics on TV. It's a great world event, but have you ever wondered how the games started?

Or you could start with a one-sentence paragraph:

Everybody's heard of the Olympic Games.

In the dinosaur text, there was a surprising twist in it – the bit about birds being dinosaurs. As you look through the facts below, you might find a surprise there that you could use to finish your writing with.

The Olympic Games

● The words 'Citius, Altius, Fortius' are written under the five rings. They mean, 'Quicker, Higher, Stronger'.
● Most important event was the foot-race in the stadium.
● First record of Olympic Games: 776 BC. Open-air stadium seated 40,000.
● Many events: foot-races, wrestling, boxing, horse racing, chariot racing with mules, long jump, spear throwing, discus, races for soldiers clad in full armour, four-horse chariot races.
● Men only. All competitors naked for most events. Strictly no women allowed.
● Women had own games a few miles away.
● Greeks not impressed by luck. Wanted to see men triumph over great odds.
● Main aim to select one man who had 'the magic of victory'.
● Special events for boys.
● When the victor returned to home town, didn't go through gate; they knocked wall down because he was a conqueror.
● Some people criticised the games as 'a public nuisance'. Said athletes were 'spoilt and over admired'. Of little use as soldiers in war and no good as advisers in peace.
● Special procession afterwards, for male victor and female victor in chariot together (both with their clothes on, of course!).
● One woman, Pherenike, trained her son for the boys' races but didn't trust the ordinary trainers. Disguised herself as a man in order to coach him in the stadium. Boy won. She gave herself away in her excitement. Tried for a serious crime but let off with a caution.
● Roman Emperor Theodosius abolished games a thousand years later (AD 393) because they were not Christian.

UNIT FIVE: *Finding The Bismarck*

TEXT: FROM *EXPLORING THE BISMARCK* BY ROBERT D. BALLARD (HODDER & STOUGHTON, 1991)

Reading

Robert Ballard, the man who found the wreck of the Titanic, also discovered the wreck of a famous German warship of the Second World War, the Bismarck. His own ship, the Star Hercules, was equipped with an underwater search robot fitted with video cameras. With this he could search the Atlantic Ocean floor at a great depth. The 'van' referred to in the text, is a special cabin on deck from which scientists controlled operations. Accompanying the team of explorers were three members of the Bismarck's crew who survived the sinking.

Read the text and summarise it in no more than three or four sentences.

Finding the Bismarck

We were about to take our first look at the mighty Bismarck, unseen by human eyes for almost fifty years. Billy Yanuck's watch was on duty in the control van, and there were quite a few spectators. No one who was awake wanted to miss the show.

'All right, let's see what kind of shape she's in,' I said. 'Billy, go down slowly.'

Billy pushed forward on the joystick and the altitude reading began to decrease: 50 metres, 45 metres, 40 metres, 35 metres.

We were coming in directly over the wreck, like a helicopter dropping down over an enemy position. About 30 metres from the bottom a ghostly gray form materialized dimly in the murky distance.

'Okay, bring her down gently.' The wind on the surface had been picking up for the past couple of hours, and the Argo was rising and falling as much as several metres with each swell. The last thing I needed right now was a crash landing.

Gradually the murk thinned and the details of the picture on the video monitors came into focus. First we saw an undamaged gun turret, then horribly mangled metal plating where a shell had hit.

Our goal was to videotape and photograph every inch of the sunken ship. As the hours passed, a clearer picture of the wreck began to emerge. It was a strange mixture of destruction and preservation. Many guns were still in place, but there were some huge holes in the deck and some of the upper parts of the ship had been completely blasted away.

continued

As we approached the rear gunnery control station I sensed the anticipation in the van. We had all read the Bismarck story and we knew that this was where Lieutenant-Commander Burkard von Mullenheim-Rechberg had spent the battle. This was also the place where so many of those who survived the sinking had sought shelter, including the three friends from the rear gunnery computer room – Adi Eich, Franz Halke and Heinz Jucknat. It was amazing that the station had survived the battle so well, since it was not heavily armored.

Now we headed aft, past the round gaping mouths where turrets had once sat. None of the four big turrets was still attached to the ship. Soon we were out over the empty decking and approaching the stern.

'Stop! What's that?' I said. Argo's video cameras had just picked up some dark markings on the ship.

'It's a cross,' said a voice behind me.

'No,' I said. 'No, that's not a cross. It's a swastika.'

'Of course, the swastika,' someone said, half to himself.

The van went silent. In our excitement we'd forgotten just what we were looking at: a Nazi warship. Suddenly all the vile associations that went with the Nazi symbol ran through our minds: the invasions which led to the outbreak of World War Two bringing widespread death and destruction, the concentration camps and the millions of people murdered there. My mind went back to the day Hitler came on board to inspect his new battleship before her first mission.

Although the swastikas on the bow and stern decks had been painted over when the Bismarck headed for the Atlantic, after forty-eight years the sea water had gradually worn that paint away. For almost five hours we beetled our way along the deck of the ravaged ship, awed by the damage yet marvelling at how much remained, how powerful and proud the ship still looked. I wondered what the survivors would think when they saw the pictures of the Bismarck again after so long.

Discussion

Make sure you have summarised the text in writing before you start this section.

1   What similarities and differences are there between the story of the Bismarck and the story of the Titanic? Is there anybody who doesn't know the story of the Titanic?

2   What excites the explorers to start with, and why has their mood changed at the end of the text?

3   How do you think survivors would have felt on seeing the Bismarck again on videotape?

Words and Spelling

1 The finding of the Bismarck was very dependent on modern technology. List all the technological words used, for example: control van, joystick, altitude reading etc.

2 Select one or two words that describe what the sea was like, and three or four words and phrases describing the damage to the Bismarck.

3 The author uses two ANTONYMS (opposites) to describe the ship: 'a mixture of destruction and preservation'. Write down an example of the destruction and an example of the preservation.

4 Write down some more antonyms that you can think of. Start with five easy ones like 'big/little', 'hard/soft', and then think of two that are a bit more like 'destruction/preservation'.

> Antonyms are not always exactly opposite but will be opposite in lots of ways. There is not always only one antonym. For example, the opposite of 'destruction' could also be 'construction' or 'reconstruction' or 'restoration'. It is very handy, having a number of words to choose from. You could, for example, say that David was small, while his opponent Goliath was 'huge', 'gigantic', 'enormous' or 'colossal'. It's a way of writing a contrast that the reader can see vividly. You can choose the effect you want.

5 In the text, what is the word that triggers off the writer's thoughts about war? What does the word mean, and where does it come from?

6 What do you think the phrase 'vile associations' means?

7 This text was written by an American, and he uses two American English spellings. Which are they?

8 What else is there that feels like American English? Look at some of the writer's expressions.

9 Explain the phrase 'half to himself'. Why should the speaker say it only half to himself? Who do you think it might have been? The text doesn't tell you.

Grammar and Punctuation

1 In the first paragraph, there is one adjective that describes the ship, and three in the last paragraph. Find them and write them down. One of the adjectives is almost an antonym of the other three; which one is it?

2 Find the statement 'None of the four big turrets was still attached to the ship'. Explain why it says 'None . . . was attached' and not 'none were attached'.

Some people do say 'none were' but it is considered non-standard English. What does 'none' mean?

To help you, look at the sentence at the end of the first paragraph, 'No one who was awake wanted to miss the show'. It is not likely that anyone would say 'No one were . . .', is it?

3 Collect together all the words in the 'one' and 'body' family, for example: no one, anybody, everyone, someone etc. Are they singular words or plural? Do they take a singular or plural verb form?

4 Some people argue that the 'body' in 'everybody' could be male or female, so there must be at least two. Therefore, 'everybody must have their say' is now correct. What do you think?

5 Write sentences containing the words 'either' and 'neither'. Are they singular or plural? What verb form do they take?

Making sure that the number and the verb are right is called **agreement**.

E.g. She (one person) runs (singular verb form)
They (more than one) run (plural verb form)

6 In three places in the text, a colon is used to punctuate two parts of a sentence. Find them and look closely at where the colon has been placed. What does the colon do in each sentence?

Write a description for a dictionary, explaining what colons are used for.

7 The sentence beginning, 'Billy pushed forward', ends with a list of measurements. Why do you think the author has done it this way?

8 Find the following sentence openings:
- About 30 metres from the bottom . . .
- Gradually . . .
- As the hours passed . . .
- As we approached the rear gunnery control station . . .
- Although the swastikas on the bow and stern decks had been painted over when the Bismarck headed for the Atlantic . . .

They all lead up to the main point of the sentence.
Write four sentences of your own, using these key opening words:

- 'About . . .'
- 'Gradually . . .'
- 'As . . .'
- 'Although . . .'

Make sure your opener leads up to the main thing you want to say.

Your own writing

The piece of writing you are going to produce in this unit is something that could go in a history magazine or in an encyclopedia. Here are your instructions:

1   Write the story of the Bismarck as told by one of the three survivors, Adi, Franz or Heinz. You choose which one, and write in the first person as though he is telling the story.

2   More information about the Bismarck is listed below. There are also some memories of the sinking, told by the three sailors. Use this information, plus your own summary of the account of how the sunken Bismarck was discovered and tell the whole story from 1939 to 1989. Your own summary will obviously be the final part, though you may have to alter it a bit to make it fit in.

Don't just copy out the notes in section A below; rewrite them to sound like a story being told by Adi, Franz or Heinz. Section B contains personal memories. You don't have to use all of them.

A

- 4 February, 1939: Bismarck launched as thousands cheer and give Nazi salute.
- 5 May, 1941: Hitler inspected Bismarck; visited gunnery computer room where Adi, Franz and Heinz were on duty; put his hands on Heinz's and Adi's shoulders.
- 19 May, 1941: Bismarck sets sail from Gotenhafen in Poland to sink merchant ships in Atlantic.
- 21 May, 1941: Spitfire flies near Bismarck in Norwegian fjord; takes photographs.
- 24 May, 1941: British send pride of the fleet, HMS Hood but battle lasts only minutes; Hood blown up.
- 26 May, 1941: Bismarck spotted again by RAF flying boat; later that night an RAF Swordfish fires a torpedo and jams Bismarck's rudder; ship could no longer be steered.
- 27 May, 1941: British ships closed in and sank Bismarck; hundreds of sailors in the water; 115 men survived out of a crew of 2,206; Adi, Franz and Heinz ended up in prisoner-of-war camp in Canada.

B

'Attention seamen of the Bismarck, this is your captain. We have just learned that the Fuhrer plans to inspect our ship before we embark on our mission. We have less than twenty-four hours to prepare for him. Go to your battle stations immediately where you will receive further instructions.' (loudspeaker announcement)

'The chief engineer ordered us to scuttle. This was the one order I prayed we would never hear. It meant filling the ship with water so that it sank as quickly as possible.' (Heinz)

'I wanted to go back to my quarters to get my belongings but there was no time.' (Franz)

'Heinz climbed up a cable shaft to get to safety. Franz and I followed him.' (Adi)

'There was an explosion and yellow smoke filled the room. I had lost my gas mask and was coughing badly. Heinz ripped one off a dead man and gave it to me.' (Franz)

'We needed to get to a lower deck but the stairs were gone. Franz was afraid to jump. 'I'll break my leg', he said. 'Better to break your leg than lose your life', I said, and we jumped. I landed on a dead body, Franz on a sack of potatoes.' (Adi)

'We were in the water for about an hour, and then a British cruiser picked us up.' (Adi)

'The water was icy cold, but far worse than the cold was the fuel oil that got into your eyes and lungs.' (Heinz)

'I tried to grab a line but couldn't so I swam to another ship but it took three tries to get me aboard. One poor devil had lost both his arms and tried to hold on to the rope with his teeth. But it was no good, he drowned.' (Franz)

'I finally made it on board and a friendly sailor handed me a bottle of rum. I was violently sick but at least it got the oil out of my stomach. They took me to an infirmary and there was Adi.' (Heinz)

UNIT SIX: *Secret Language*

TEXT: BASED ON *SPHINX*, A BRITISH GOVERNMENT CIPHER USED A HUNDRED YEARS AGO.

Reading: Instructions for using Sphinx

The Sphinx Cipher is based on a keyword, chosen by, and known only by, the parties concerned (see below).

	A	B	C	D	E	F	G	H	i	J	K	L	M	N	O	P	Q	R	S	T	U	V	W	X	Y	Z
M	b	c	d	e	f	g	h	i	j	k	l	m	n	o	p	q	r	s	t	u	v	w	x	y	z	a
I	c	d	e	f	g	h	i	j	k	l	m	n	o	p	q	r	s	t	u	v	w	x	y	z	a	b
C	d	e	f	g	h	i	j	k	l	m	n	o	p	q	r	s	t	u	v	w	x	y	z	a	b	c
H	e	f	g	h	i	j	k	l	m	n	o	p	q	r	s	t	u	v	w	x	y	z	a	b	c	d
A	f	g	h	i	j	k	l	m	n	o	p	q	r	s	t	u	v	w	x	y	z	a	b	c	d	e
E	g	h	i	j	k	l	m	n	o	p	q	r	s	t	u	v	w	x	y	z	a	b	c	d	e	f
L	h	i	j	k	l	m	n	o	p	q	r	s	t	u	v	w	x	y	z	a	b	c	d	e	f	g

How To Use Sphinx

1 Look at the way the alphabet has been arranged in the table above. The first row contains the complete alphabet, the other horizontal rows each begin one letter further on in the alphabet. The vertical columns also follow an alphabetic sequence.

2 Look at the column on the extreme left of the table. This would be blank to start off with.

3 Insert a seven-letter word in the first column. Ensure that each letter is a different one. This word must be kept TOP SECRET.

4 Let the word be the name MICHAEL for demonstration purposes. This is now the keyword of the cipher.

5 Suppose that the message you want to send is:
COVER BLOWN GET OUT FAST.

6 Match the message with the keyword as follows, repeating the keyword over and over again:

COVER	BLOWN	GET	OUT	FAST
MICHA	ELMIC	HAE	LMI	CHAE

7 Now look for the first letter of your message, which is C, in the top horizontal row of the table.

8 Next find the first letter of the keyword column (M in this example) and

continued

read along the alphabet horizontally until you come to the letter under the first letter of your message (C in this example). You will find the letter d.

9 Repeat the above with the second letter of your message and your keyword until you have encoded the whole message.

10 The whole message should now read:

dqyiw   hspyq   kjz   vvv   iexz

11 To decode a message, write the keyword underneath the encoded message and reverse the proceeding:

This first two words of the message have been done below.

d q y i w	Md	=	capital C
M I C H A	Iq	=	capital O
	Cy	=	capital V
	Hi	=	capital E
	Aw	=	capital R
h s p y q	Eh	=	capital B
E L M I C	Ls	=	capital L
	Mp	=	capital O
	Iy	=	capital W
	Cq	=	capital N

12 The keyword may be changed at any time by prior agreement.

13 For longer messages keep repeating the keyword until you have encoded all the message.

14 MEMORISE THESE INSTRUCTIONS AND DESTROY.

Good instructions should always be to the point and as brief as possible. There is therefore, no need to summarise this text.

Discussion

1 It is to be hoped that you haven't taken the second half of instruction 14 literally, or you won't be able to read this!
Codes and ciphers have been around since Ancient Egyptian times. They were used in the Middle Ages, Queen Elizabeth I and Shakespeare used them, and they have been used in war, government and business right up until today. Why do people need them?

2 Make sure you have understood the instructions. Do you think The Sphinx is a good code? Have you come across it before? It was used in the First World War and also appears in John Buchan's *Thirty Nine Steps*.

3 Explain why it is that three letters in the message can have the same code symbol (V) yet it is still possible to decode them accurately.

Words and Spelling

1 Look up the words 'cipher' and 'code'. You will find some similarities. Are there any differences in meaning? Notice how they can both have 'de' and 'en' added to them: decipher, encode.

Put together the word family for 'code'. (Don't forget your postcode!)

2 The word 'key' is also an interesting one that has a number of meanings. Look up the word in a decent-sized dictionary and you will find a large entry. Look out also for the following:

keystone,   keyboard,
key signature,   key money,
key grip,   keynote

Also find out in geography, where islands and reefs are called 'keys'.

3 Everybody knows what an ordinary, everyday key is: it's a metal thing for locking and unlocking doors. That is the **literal meaning** of the word. 'Literal' means 'actual'. At the beginning of the discussion section, it was hoped that you hadn't 'literally' i.e. 'actually' destroyed the page on which the code instructions were written.

Often, ordinary words are not used in literal ways. Look at the following sentences:

> He drowned in his sorrows.
> She flew downstairs to answer the phone.
> I fell for the girl/boy next door.
> We shot them down in flames. (i.e. won the argument)

None of these sentences is literally true. They could be, but it is highly unlikely. He didn't actually drown. She didn't really fly. I didn't really fall. We weren't actually engaged in aerial warfare. They are all figures of speech. The technical term for them is METAPHOR. They have **metaphorical meaning**, not literal meaning.

> We use metaphors all the time, often without thinking. The meaning of one thing is added to the meaning of another.

4 Imagine what school life would be like if the following were literally true:

The English teacher split her sides and her pupils fell apart laughing.
The school secretary has been in a spin all day.
Steam was coming out of the head's ears at assembly this morning.
The maths teachers have all flipped their lids.

The school orchestra has just raised the roof.
The whole of Year Nine has gone bananas.
The school governors are on the war-path.
The caretaker lives in cloud cuckoo land.
The school toilets are a pig sty.
The school inspectors are going over everything with a fine-tooth comb.
None of these things can be literally true, but they are sayings that add meaning and colour to the things people say. Humans do not like language to be plain and literal all the time.

Explain what the following metaphors mean:

- Split her sides . . . fell apart
- In a spin
- Steam coming out of his ears
- Flipped their lids
- Going over things with a fine tooth comb
- Gone bananas
- On the war-path
- Cloud cuckoo land
- A pig sty
- Raising the roof

Our minds are full of metaphors just waiting to be used. We often don't even notice we are using them. Just keep an eye and an ear open over the next week or two for things that can't be literally true, but which are meant metaphorically. You will often have a good laugh to yourself, as when somebody says, 'My feet are killing me'.

5   There is an old pop song called 'For all we know' sung by Nat King Cole. In it there's a line: 'I'll hold out my hand, and my heart will be in it'. It's actually a very romantic song but if you take these words literally, it sounds like a horror movie!

The word 'heart' is often used metaphorically: she broke my heart (oops!); lift up your hearts; he has a heavy heart; I give you my heart (ugh!); my heart stood still; put your heart into it; I left my heart in San Francisco (how careless of you!); have a heart (thank you very much!); a heart-to-heart talk.

Other parts of the body are also spoken of metaphorically: fish fingers; two heads are better than one; she won by a short head; will you foot the bill?; the factory hands are on strike; he's giving you the eye; in my mind's eye; let me bend your ear; you can't palm me off with rubbish.

Choose two body-parts and think of as many metaphorical uses as you can. Write them in sentences.

   'Head' and 'foot' are good ones to investigate.

6 The keyword of the Sphinx cipher 'unlocks' the secret message.
The word 'key' and the word for the thing it opens, 'lock', are often used metaphorically. It is because the ideas of a key and a lock are very vivid but also very familiar. Here are some examples. Explain what they mean.

- I've got the key to all your troubles.
- They were locked in mortal combat.
- I'd like to unlock some of the mysteries of the universe.
- She is a key person in the school.
- We're all keyed up to go.
- Have you got a key to all these symbols on the map?
- I wish I had the key to unlock your heart.
- The keystone of a building locks together all the other stones in an arch.

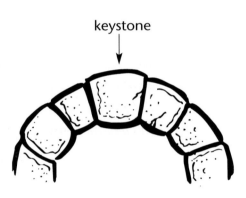

keystone

7 When you looked up the word 'cipher' in the dictionary, did it also tell you that the word can be spelt 'cypher' if you wish? English does not have a lot of alternative spellings, but that is one of them.

8 The origin of the word 'alphabet' is an interesting one. It is made up of the names for the first two letters of the Greek alphabet: 'alpha' = 'a' and 'beta' = 'b'. Some other names for Greek letters are also used in English: 'gamma', 'delta' and 'omega'. Where might you have seen these words? If you haven't noticed any of them, keep an eye open. A radiation science, a credit card and delivery service will give you some clues.

9 What does the phrase 'prior agreement' mean?

10 What does the word 'Sphinx' mean? Where does it come from? What makes it particularly suitable as a name for a code?
Another codename you may have heard of is 'Enigma'. This was a code machine the German navy used in World War Two to communicate secretly with submarines. The word 'Enigma' is also particularly suitable as the name of a code. Look up its meaning.

Sometimes the word 'enigmatic' is used to describe a person, for example: 'She has a very enigmatic look on her face.' There is something very enigmatic about 'the little furry girl' in *Playing Beatie Bow* (see Unit 10). What do you think the word means?

Grammar and Punctuation

The main purpose of instructions is to tell people what they have to do.

> The keywords in instructions are the IMPERATIVE VERBS. Imperative verbs tell you what to do. They are also called 'commands' (for obvious reasons) and 'directives' because they direct people.

Sometimes, in instructions, you also have to include helpful information, and adverbs such as 'now' and 'next'. Instructions sometimes need adverbs like 'slowly', 'carefully', 'gently', 'firmly', but these are not suitable here. They might be suitable in bicycle repair instructions, for example.

1 Look at the first nine instructions in the text. All of them, except two, begin with the same kind of word. What kind of word is it? What does it do? What kind of word do the two exceptions begin with? Why? What do you notice about the word which follows them?
What kind of sentences are 10 and 12?

2 Of the remaining five in the list (10–14), two give you instructions and three give you information. Which are which?

3 Instructions 3, 8 and 14, contain two imperative verbs each; what are the second ones?

4 The layout of instructions can be called a format. A format is a usual way in which things are set out so that people will know what to expect. Make a list of all the things that the following would have in common:

recipes, washing machine operating instructions, how to play a game, software instructions.

Your own writing

Write a set of instructions for something you know how to use. It could be another kind of code, but it could be something quite different, for example: a computer game, loading a film, sending an e-mail.
Whatever you choose, your main task is to instruct a reader how to do it.
Take your time thinking about what to do, and make sure you know yourself, what you are doing.
If you look at the instructions for using the Sphinx Cipher, you will see that everything necessary has been provided: the alphabetical table, information as well as instructions, and an example. Whatever you choose to write instructions for, make sure they are just as helpful.
Choose your imperative verbs carefully, and think about any adverbs you may need, especially those ending in 'ly'. If you don't want your reader to break something delicate, remember words like 'carefully', 'lightly' and 'gently'.

UNIT SEVEN: *Aliens*

TEXT: FROM *THE NEXT 500 YEARS* **BY ADRIAN BERRY (HEADLINE, 1996) CHAPTER 19.**

Reading (adapted from original)

The following text comes from a book about what life may be like in the third millennium. It consists of extremely knowledgeable guesswork based on available scientific evidence and on researches already in progress. It prophesises for example, intensive farming of the seas, the mining of asteroids for industrial resources, the colonisation of Mars and the storage of human personalities on computer discs for retrieval after death. More disastrous, are the possibilities of another Ice Age or of humans being taken over by super-intelligent robots. All these are based on scientific fact; they are not just science fiction.

Read the text and summarise its main points in one (or two) sentences. Before reading it however, make sure you understand the meanings of the following words and phrases:

'available scientific evidence', 'researches', 'prophesise' (a verb, but notice that as a noun it is spelt 'prophecies' – what's the difference?), 'intensive farming', 'asteroids', 'industrial resources', 'colonisation', 'retrieval'.

Have we got company?

Far and few, far and few,
Are the lands where the Jumblies live;
Their heads are green, and their hands are blue,
And they went to sea in a Sieve.
>(from *The Jumblies* by Edward Lear)

Within 500 years, and probably in much less time, we should know whether ours is the only advanced technological society in our Milky Way galaxy. It is probably also safe to assert that the discovery of an alien civilisation will affect the way we think and behave more than any other possible scientific discovery. A rival civilisation would look upon the galaxy, or any part of it, in exactly the same way as our descendants will, as property to be conquered. Unfortunately, if another civilisation is discovered, the chances are that its technology will be superior to ours.

If other civilisations were inferior to our own, we should have no way of detecting their presence since they would not yet have invented radio. As for their being our approximate equals, the probability of that is very low. In the ten

---

continued

billion years since the galaxy was formed, it is unlikely that two civilisations could arise with parallel histories, both discovering radio, electronics and rocketry in the same century. That only leaves the possibility that they will be thousands, or even millions, of years in advance of us.

What would they be like? They could not be human – that is far too improbable – but would they be human-like? Would their bodies be based, like ours, on oxygen and carbon, or on some totally unknown arrangement of elements? Having multi-fingered hands, two eyes, two ears, a mouth and a nose seems to us very efficient, but can better organs be adapted in better ways? We cannot know any more than the Dutch astronomer Christian Huygens who wrote in the 17th century:

> 'Were we to meet with a creature of a much different shape from Man, with reason and speech, we should be much surprised and shocked at the sight. We might try to imagine or paint a creature like a man in everything else, but with a neck four times as long, and great round eyes five or six times as big, though we could not look upon it without the utmost horror.'

Whatever they looked like, because of their technical superiority we should be as helpless in the face of their machines, as people of the Stone Age would be in the face of ours today.

Despite their superiority, there is no guarantee whatever that another civilisation would be benevolent. H G Wells, who wrote the science fiction classic, 'War of the Worlds', once said that if alien beings claimed that their sole wish was to 'serve' mankind, we should ask ourselves most seriously whether that means they wish to serve us fried or baked.

But there are no signs of aliens anywhere in the galaxy or on Earth. Everywhere scientists look with their radio telescopes, whatever spectrum they use, whether radio, optical, infra-red, ultaviolet or gamma ray, they cannot find anything but 'natural' noise, the everlasting and meaningless chaos emitted by the stars. There is as yet no evidence whatever – apart from the microbes that men and their instruments take with them when they explore other planets – of life, in any form, existing beyond the Earth.

In 1993, NASA began a $10 million a year project called 'The Search for Extra Terrestrial Intelligence' (SETI). One day, it might announce that they have found unmistakable artificial signals coming from a planet circling Proxima Centauri, the closest star to the Sun. If these signals were confirmed, the sensational news would cover the front pages of every newspaper in the world.

I have taken bets that this will not happen, despite being offered very poor odds. We don't have company in the universe. There will be no invasion from outer space, and there will be no opposition when we eventually occupy other worlds. Every planet that we find will be ours by right of conquest.

This is quite a long text to summarise. Try to do it in four sentences.

Discussion

1 Of the various things that the author of this text says, what interests you most? Do you agree or disagree with anything?

2 Is he writing about science fiction or something else?

3 Discuss some of the different ways people you know might react if an alien called round one evening. What problems might there be? How would you react? Don't be afraid to use your imagination.

Words and Spelling

1 Check the meanings of the following words:

> assert, reason, superiority, benevolent, utmost, chaos, Terrestrial, confirmed.

2 The words above have been used in the following sentences, but the sentences are not complete. Complete the sentences to show that you know the meanings of the words underlined. Sometimes you may have to think of the last part of the sentence, sometimes the first half. In the fourth one you have to find both the beginning and the end of a sentence!

> H G Wells <u>asserts</u> that . . .
> I cannot think of any good <u>reason</u> why . . .
> . . . because of their <u>superiority</u>.
> . . . a very <u>benevolent</u> . . .
> Please do your <u>utmost</u> to . . .
> . . . living in <u>chaos</u> like this!
> The most common <u>Terrestrial</u> creatures are . . .
> . . . <u>confirmed</u> by letter.

3 Complete the word families for the following words:

> assert, reason, superiority (don't just put any word beginning with 'super'), confirmed.

'Super' is also used as a prefix. List some examples.

4 Which language do the following words come from?

> benevolent, Terrestrial, universe, intelligence.

5 Which language does the word 'chaos' come from?
How alien is the word 'alien', and where does it come from?

6 'Proxima Centauri' and 'Milky Way' are both astronomical terms that come from different languages. Which are the two languages?

7 Look for the phrases '"natural" noise' and 'artificial signals'. Explain the difference in your own words. What is so special about the word 'artificial'?

8 Find out, if you do not know, what radio, optical, infra-red, ultraviolet and gamma rays are. If you do know, write an explanation for someone who doesn't.

9 See if you can find any of the following words in the text:

probably, possible, if, unlikely, possibility.

What do words like this tell you? Why do we need them?
What is the difference in meaning between 'possible' and 'probable'?

10 Use the text as a basis for a spelling test, making sure your partner cannot look at it. Choose some words (five to ten) and see if your partner can spell them properly.
Then let your partner test you.

Grammar and Punctuation

1 The text begins with a quotation from another text by Edward Lear. What is the point of this?

2 Later in the text there are quotations from Christian Huygens and H G Wells. One is an indirect quotation (reported speech), the other is a direct quotation (direct speech). Which is which? How do you know?

Rewrite each one so that the direct speech is reported and the indirect is made direct. Make sure your punctuation is accurate.

3 Which idea interests you most: Huygens' or Wells'? If you agree with one of them or both, write why in about three sentences. If you disagree with one of them, or both, write why.

4 What pronoun does the text begin with and how many times is that pronoun used? What other pronoun goes with it?

5 What pronoun does the text end with? Look at the beginning of the last paragraph. Why has the author shifted to another pronoun?

6 The author says that an alien civilisation could be different from ours in three ways. Find the paragraph in which he does this and write out the opening words of the sentences that tell you about the differences.

7 Scan the text very carefully and count the number of times the following words are used:

should, would, could, can, cannot, might.

Write down the number of times each word is used and then add them all up.
What do the words do to what is being said?
What does it mean when writers use these particular words?

8 The words you have just been exploring belong to a small group of English words of Old English origin that people use all the time. Others in this group are:

> must,   may,   ought to,   need to,
> (and the negatives: must not, may not, ought not, need not).

> These are called **modal verbs** because they go in front of other verbs to make their meaning less definite or certain.

Look at the examples you have just found, and list the verbs that follow them. When you are not sure about what will happen, when you are guessing or predicting, modal verbs help you to express your uncertainty: it *may* happen, it *can* break, it *should* do the trick, it *ought* to work, you *need not* go, I *might* lend it to you.

You can also use them to express politeness but also to persuade. Look at the following pairs of sentences:

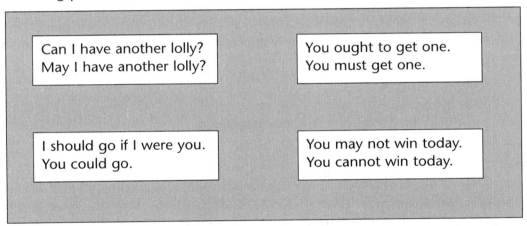

Can I have another lolly?
May I have another lolly?

You ought to get one.
You must get one.

I should go if I were you.
You could go.

You may not win today.
You cannot win today.

Explain the differences between these pairs. Work with a partner and say them to each other. Listen to the tone of voice you use for each one.

Look now, at the last paragraph of the text. Are there any modal verbs in it? If not, why not?

9 In the text there is a sentence beginning with the word 'But'. This is a turning point in what the author is saying. Explain in your own written words, what the big 'But' is. He is very sure of himself. Do you agree with him? If you don't, write him a short letter explaining why you disagree.

10 Find the following three punctuations:

● – that is far too improbable –
● 'natural'
● human-like

What do the dashes do in the first one? Look at their place in the whole sentence. Is this kind of punctuation used anywhere else in the text?
It is a way of slipping into a sentence an extra bit of information. The technical term for it is **parenthesis**. You can also use commas or brackets for the same effect. Write out each of the sentences twice, using brackets in one version and commas in the other. Discuss with a partner if there is any difference, and which you prefer.

You have already looked at the inverted commas used to indicate a direct quotation from the Dutch astronomer Huygens. The inverted commas on the word 'natural' are not doing the same job at all. Why are they there?

Notice the hyphen in 'human-like'. Why do you think it is there?
Write out three sentences of your own in which you have used a hyphen plus 'like' in this way, for example: egg-like, fish-like, banana-like, pen-like.

Your own writing

The text you have just been studying is about possibilities – what COULD happen, what MIGHT be – which is one reason why there are so many modal verbs. The author cannot know for sure. You may think his view is a bit pessimistic or negative.

You now have the choice of two pieces of writing. One is a reply to the author saying what you think, or you could write your own view of what might happen in the future without referring to his text at all. Whichever you choose, you will have to do two things that the author did:

1   You will have to use modal verbs and words such as 'probably', 'unlikely', 'if', 'possible' and 'probable', because you can be no more certain than Berry is. You are entitled to your opinion though, so don't be afraid to use your imagination.
    Adverbs like 'probably', 'likely' and 'unlikely', enable you to say something without committing yourself, which is why they are called QUALIFIERS; they qualify what you have said. The same is true of adjectives like 'probable' and 'possible'. A word like 'if' automatically signals that there is a condition to whatever you are going to say or whatever is coming next.

2   You will also have to introduce what you have to say, and put the different possibilities into paragraphs. When you have written about some possibilities, end with a paragraph about what you personally believe.

Make sure you have given your writing a good title, and see if you can find a quotation from somewhere that you can put at the beginning of your writing, for example, from Star Trek or from a book you know.

UNIT EIGHT: *A Matter of Life and Death*

TEXT: **THE TWO ARGUMENTS BELOW HAVE BEEN ADAPTED FROM** *SOLO: BOOK 3,* **A SERIES OF MONOLOGUES FOR DRAMA IN ENGLISH BY JOHN GOODWIN AND BILL TAYLOR, (HODDER & STOUGHTON EDUCATIONAL, 1996)**

Readings: Arguments for and against the death penalty

Esmonde Willis is 24 years old. He has been sentenced to death by lethal injection, for the killing of a shopkeeper, George Schwitzer. Since then he has been waiting on Death Row.

The first text is a pamphlet campaigning against the death penalty. The second is a pamphlet on behalf of a group called 'Families Against Evil' who support death sentences for murder.

Read the two texts, summarising each one in a separate sentence.

Abolish the death penalty

There is no doubt that Esmonde Willis is a disturbed young man. He has been diagnosed as deeply paranoid.

There is also no doubt that he can be violent. On several occasions he has even threatened his defense attorney with violence when an appeal went against him.

So why fight to save him?

The answer is simple – JUSTICE.

That Esmonde murdered George Schwitzer is not in dispute. Because of his mental condition, everybody agrees that he is never likely to be rehabilitated into society.

But neither of these things justify the taking of his life.

If we believe in a moral code we must be prepared to take responsibility for that code when someone breaks it.

Although that code says that killing is wrong, evil, barbarous and inhuman, we nevertheless punish murder with a death sentence. Moreover, we claim to be following the Bible in doing this: an eye for an eye, a life for a life. But this is not justice; it is revenge.

An execution is an act of revenge. An execution is another murder.

Therefore, campaign against the execution of Esmonde Willis.

Keep the death penalty

Esmonde Willis walked into a drugstore and demanded money at gunpoint. When the storekeeper, George Schwitzer refused, Willis shot him dead. George Schwitzer was 42. He leaves a wife with three children and another on the way. Willis destroyed the lives of six people, yet there was less than 200 dollars in the till.

Are you going to say that that's defensible? That Esmonde Willis had had a bad childhood? That his mother hated him? That he wasn't very bright at school? That he didn't mean it?
Because of these things, are you going to say that he is a special case?
NO, you are not.

Until we see things for what they are, nothing is going to change.

You want your family to live in a society where you can drive down the street and not have to keep a gun under your seat. You want to walk through a shopping mall and not have to worry that someone coming toward you might be a psychopath.

If we want that security, we have to execute murderers.

Despite the evil in the world, there is also good. People know what is right and what is wrong.
But God gave us the gift of free will, which means that we can choose evil or good. So you make the choice and you pay the price.

Esmonde Willis, therefore, should pay the price for the evil he has done.

Discussion

Make sure you have summarised in writing each of the arguments before you start this section.

1   Britain has abolished the death penalty, though there are still campaigners for re-introducing it. Some American states, and many countries in the world, still enforce the death penalty.
    What is your view? Which of the two texts persuades you the most?

2   What are 'psychopaths', and would the death penalty protect people from them?

3   Is there anything in either of these arguments that plays on your feelings?

Words and Spelling

1   Write a dictionary entry for the word 'sentence'. You will need to do it in two parts because there are at least two different meanings.
    DO NOT look at a dictionary until you have written your own definition.

How is the word being used in this text?

2 Look up the meanings of the following words you are not sure about:

- abolish
- lethal
- paranoid
- dispute
- campaign.

3 The word 'rehabilitated' is quite a long one, as are other members of its family (rehabilitation, rehabilitates, rehabilitating). It is made up of three bits (re + habilit + ated). You will know that the 'ated' bit is to do with the past tense, and you probably know what 're' means at the beginning of a word. But what does the middle bit mean? And what does the whole word mean in this text?

Here are some more words built up in the same way:

| renovated | reactivated | reciprocated | recapitulated |
| spiflicated | recuperated | refrigerated | reverberated. |

Long aren't they? Make sure you can pronounce them, but don't be afraid of them.
Split each one into its three bits, and find out/work out what the middle bit means. Then you will be able to work out what the whole word means. What do you think 'ated' means?

4 What on earth is the difference between a 'moral code' and a secret code? You looked at a secret code in Unit 6. What does 'moral' mean?

5 Another interesting word in the first text is 'revenge'. It belongs to quite a big family. Find the other members. Where do the words 'avenge' and 'avengers' fit in?

6 One word and the spelling of the one before it may have given you an immediate clue that this text is American (see the second paragraph of 'Abolish the Death Penalty'). What are the words? Find out the meaning of one of the words and the English spelling of the other.

English is now a world language, though what we should say is that there are many different Englishes in the world today. British English is the parent but we can no longer say that British English is the only correct one. Its children have grown up in vastly different parts of the world and developed their own ways of doing things, as all children should. Some things don't change, but others do.

There are seven families of English throughout the world; each family has other families within it.

a) *British English* (including English English, Scottish English, Welsh English, Irish English);

b) *American English* (including N. American English, S. American English, Appalachian English);

c) *Canadian English* (including Canadian Standard English, Atlantic Provinces English, Inuit English);

d) *Caribbean English* (including Patwa English, Jamaican English, Trinidadian English, Bahamian English etc.);

e) *African English* (including Nigerian English, Ghanaian English, East African English, South African English);

f) *East Asian English* (including Philippines English, Hawaiian English, Malayan English, Singapore English, etc.);

g) *Australian/New Zealand English* (including Maori English, Aboriginal English, etc.).

Check that you know where these places are on a world map. The words 'Inuit' and 'Maori' refer to people. Who are they?

Everybody knows from American films and TV entertainment what the American words are for some English words: sidewalk = pavement; hood (car) = bonnet; ice-box = fridge; sneakers = trainers; attorney = solicitor.
Lots of American expressions also find their way into everyday British English: no-way; chill out; the bottom line.

American English spelling differs from British English spelling most noticably in three kinds of word endings. Sort the American English spellings given below into three lists according to their endings:

theater, defense, color, fiber, pretense, center, labor, offense, vigor, license.

Now write the British English spellings alongside them.
An American dictionary like Webster's will give both American and British English spellings.

7 Having made a start on a particular set of word endings, investigate the following, using a dictionary to check your spellings. Forget American English spellings and concentrate now on British English:

a) Collect together the word family for 'defence'. Take 'defend' as the root word.
List words where the 'c' is replaced by an 's'. Then list words where it is replaced by a 'd'.
Now see if the same patterns occur in the 'offence' word family. Take 'offend' as the root word.

b) Look at the following words ending in 're': centre, theatre, fibre, metre.
Construct the word families for any two of these words. Make sure you get the biggest possible family gathering. Compare what happens to the final 'e' when something is added to the word.

Find two or three other words ending with 're'. Do they follow a similar rule?

c) Look at these three words ending in 'our': colour, labour, vigour. Construct the word family for 'colour'.

Now get as many of the family together as you can for the words 'labour' and 'vigour'.

What happens to the 'u' when changes are made to the end of the word? Does it happen exactly the same for all three words?

Grammar and Punctuation

1

> Texts that are full of facts, figures and nouns that you can see, hear and touch, are said to be more CONCRETE than other kinds of texts.

Why does the second text seem more 'concrete' than the first? Count the concrete nouns.

Both texts though, contain ABSTRACT NOUNS because they are arguing about ideas as well as events.

> A lot of abstract nouns stand for important ideas – things that people argue about a great deal. But because abstract nouns have so many different meanings, they can be very vague until you explain them.

Some abstract nouns in the first text are not too vague. Most people have a good idea of what is meant by: an appeal, dispute, murder.

The following ones though, need a lot more explanation: violence, justice, society, moral code (there's an adjective in front of this one), responsibility, evil, revenge.

Look at the second text and list some abstract nouns that you think need explanation. Are there any that are used in the first text?

Add the ones you have found to the list above and then choose two from the combined list. They could be opposites (antonyms) like 'good' and 'evil' or 'right' and 'wrong', or they could just be different, like 'justice' and 'revenge' or 'violence' and 'moral code'.

One way of explaining what YOU mean by an abstract noun such as 'good' or 'evil' is to give concrete examples involving a verb or two. There's no end to the examples you can give, but the ones you choose will tell people what you think the abstract noun means. Here are some examples using abstract nouns not in the texts. Notice that the verbs are present participles (check this term, if you have forgotten it):

Love is: caring about somebody else
        kissing somebody
        giving up your last piece of chocolate

sharing a Coke
going on errands for bad-tempered grannies
cuddling a puppy (Aah!).

Loyalty is: turning up on time
speaking up for somebody who is not present
sticking with someone through thick and thin (even when you are not completely sure)
being there when you're needed
wearing the badge and the right colours
dying for your country.

Do you get the idea?

Now think about the two abstract nouns you have chosen, and write five examples of your abstract nouns in action, e.g.

> Society is everybody living together to help each other.
> Security is being able to walk home safely.

Don't forget the present participles.

2 Remind yourself of the four kinds of sentence:

statements,   questions,   commands,   exclamations.

What kind of sentence are the two titles? Who are they addressed to?
Each text asks a main question. What is it in each case?
Each text answers its question in a different way. How does each writer do it?
One text ends with a command. Which one is it and what is the command? Why end with a command?
The other text ends with a modal verb. Which one, and what is the modal verb? Why end this way?

3 Both texts are arguments. They are trying to persuade the reader to a particular point of view.
Important words in arguments are not necessarily the long, unusual ones; they are familiar, everyday words.

Look at the first argument. Read it slowly and notice each of these words and groups of words as they occur:

So . . .	. . . nevertheless . . .
Because . . .	Moreover . . .
But . . .	But . . .
If . . .	Therefore . . .
Although . . .	

Nine little words (well, fairly little) that don't seem to mean very much by themselves. You would have great difficulty finding any one of them or doing any one of them, and none of them tells you what anything is like. In other words they are not nouns, verbs or adjectives. Yet they do very important jobs in sentences.

> The nouns, verbs, adjectives and adverbs in English are called LEXICAL WORDS. There's about half a million of them in modern use! A medium-sized dictionary will cover about 300,000 lexical words. It is not difficult to imagine a lexical word even when it isn't in a sentence: ships; climbing; tasty; cheerfully.

> The words listed above are different; they are called GRAMMATICAL WORDS. This means that their job is not to stand for something that you can imagine, but to *connect* all the lexical words so that they say what you want them to say. And there are only about 200 of them! Isn't it remarkable that you only need 200 grammatical words to connect 500,000 lexical words?

Look at the following newspaper headlines. They are full of lexical words but all the connectors are missing.

You could be forgiven for expecting the news stories to be about dogs who have been put in charge of the local park, a football manager who has, rather oddly, lost his back, that Jackson is staying and Wright has gone and that the rest room staff are hopeless.

But some little words are missing that make all the difference to the meanings.

Look at the headlines, as they really appeared:

The 'in', 'off', 'if' and 'for' make all the difference. They tell you the 'ins and outs', if you like.

Now look at the following sentences and replace the missing connectors that fasten things together.

Each missing word is indicated by a dash:

a) She covered the distance __ ten seconds flat.
b) __ it rains, I always seem to be __ my raincoat.
c) Go __ see __ yourself, __ you like.
d) It won't work __ you haven't put it together properly.
e) __ they are not supposed to be good __ you, I like fish __ chips.
f) Let's go now, __ you have a better idea.
g) '__ it is useful, __ it isn't', she said, __ a rather superior way.

Now look how difficult it would be to guess right, if all the lexical words were missing and only the grammatical ones were left in. Below are some famous film titles. Can you guess which they are? Each dash stands for one word only.

i) The __ of __
ii) The __ and __
iii) __ to the __
iv) The __ of __
v) __ of the __

Your teacher will give you some answers but you may have found others that fit perfectly well.

> Some grammatical words put things in their proper place; these are called **prepositions.**

Familiar prepositions are:

in	under	over	of	from	with	by	on	off	to	up
down	into	opposite	around	without	within	through	along			
beneath among near to apart from over and above with towards against										

You know these words perfectly well; you've been using them all your life, you just didn't know what they were called.

> Other grammatical words are called **conjunctions**. They don't tell you where things are (as prepositions do), they make *connections between things*.

Some words used as conjunctions simply fasten things together tidily. The most popular ones are:

and	but	or	the	so

Other words used as conjunctions tell you something about the connection. The most popular ones are:

although	though	as	as	if	because	even	if	except	
if	in	case	in	order	to	rather	than	since	so	that	until
	till	when	whenever	where	whereas	wherever	while		

You may not use some of these, especially in writing, as often as you use the other conjunctions on the previous page.

Sometimes they occur in the middle of sentences, sometimes at the beginning.

Write out a sentence for each of these conjunctions. You will need to think of a longish sentence because it will need two ideas in it. You are also likely to need a comma. Here are some examples.

- Because you have been very naughty, you will be grounded all weekend. (So, there!)
- I will lend you my bike and my waterproofs, if you promise to take care of them.
- I will wait for you in the library, rather than stand outside in the cold.

Make sure you can see the two ideas in these examples:

> You have been naughty + you will be grounded
> I will lend my bike etc + you promise to take care etc
> I will wait + stand outside in the cold

A third group of words that have an important connecting job are the following:

Moreover	furthermore	however	therefore	nevertheless	also	next

Many of the 'ly' adverbs are also useful for connecting what you have just written with what is coming next:

Secondly	finally	consequently	surprisingly	accordingly
funnily enough (yes, this is one of them!)		inevitably		fortunately

Now, let's go back to those words in the first text:

so	because	but	if	although	nevertheless	moreover	but	therefore

They're all doing a connection job of some kind. Which ones do you think are conjunctions, and which are adverbs? Make a list of each.

All these words are like a backbone to the argument. If you say the sequence to yourself emphasising the words, and pausing between each, you can 'hear' the argument:

SO! blah blah blah blah BECAUSE blah blah blah blah BUT blah blah blah blah IF blah blah blah blah ALTHOUGH blah blah blah blah NEVERTHELESS blah blah blah blah MOREOVER (big emphasis on this one) blah blah blah blah BUT blah blah blah blah THEREFORE (even bigger emphasis on this last one) blah blah blah blah.

When you see words coming up like this (or use them yourself) you know you are reading or writing an argument of some kind.

Look at the second text and pick out in sequence the 'argument' words. Write them down. You can use the 'blah blah blah' method if you like.

Your own writing

In this unit you have looked at some of the ways in which things, ideas and what you want to say in writing can be connected. Just to remind you, here they are:

- using exactly the right preposition
- using conjunctions
- using adverbs.

The texts you looked at were both arguments taking different sides but using the same kinds of connecting words.

Your task, to complete this unit, is to write a pamphlet about the same length as the ones you have just investigated, in which you argue your point of view about something you care about very strongly. It doesn't have to be something as terrible as the death penalty; it can be something like super league soccer, or fox hunting or lowering the speed limit to save lives. You do not need to write the other point of view; just yours. Use the same kind of short paragraphs.

Think carefully before you choose your topic. It doesn't have to be based on the details of a particular piece of news, but make sure it is something you believe in and know something about. Discuss it first.

Remember you are writing a pamphlet to persuade people to agree with you.

Ask yourself the following questions:

- What are the main things I want to say? (Write them down first.)
- What order should I put them in? (Try out different ways.)
- Will it be a good idea to ask a question and then answer it?
- Will I need to use a command sentence anywhere?
- What connections do I need to make? (Give a reason? (Use 'because') Make a condition? (Use 'if').)
- Will I need any adverbs? (E.g. however, next, therefore.)

UNIT NINE: *Newspapers (Part One)*

TEXTS: TWO NEWSPAPER ACCOUNTS OF A POLITICIAN QUITTING THE GOVERNMENT

Readings

Newspapers love to write stories about war, conflict, arguments, disputes, fallings out and scandal. In this unit you are going to look at two newspaper accounts of the same event: Mo Mowlam's announcement of her intention to leave the government (September, 2000).

Both papers, *The Independent* and *The Mirror*, are sympathetic toward Mo Mowlam, one of them especially so. First, read the two accounts to get the gist of the story. When you have done that, write a sentence saying what you think is different about the two articles.

Mowlam to quit, but the whispers continue

MO MOWLAM, the most popular member of the Cabinet, stunned the political world yesterday by announcing that she would leave Parliament at the next general election.

The Cabinet Office Minister denied she had been driven out by sniping about her performance by aides of Tony Blair but confirmed that there had been a "whispering campaign" against her.

Ms Mowlam, 50, insisted her move was a personal and career decision. She said she wanted a job outside politics before she retired.

Downing Street said Ms Mowlam would remain in her ministerial post until the election and that Mr Blair believed her departure would be "a great loss to the Government and a great loss to Parliament".

However, the Prime Minister did not attempt to talk Ms Mowlam out of her decision when they met for 15 minutes at Downing Street yesterday.

BY ANDREW GRICE
Political Editor

Her move spares Mr Blair a dilemma over whether to keep her in the cabinet if he wins a second term.

Last night Blair aides cast fresh doubts over Ms Mowlam's political judgement. "The real question is why she didn't run for Mayor of London," one Downing Street insider told *The Independent*. "We asked her to do it but she said no. Three weeks later she changed her mind but it was too late because Frank Dobson had already entered the race."

Gwyneth Dunwoody, a senior Labour backbencher, said it was "extremely sad" that it appeared "that there were people at the top who are frightened of powerful women ... [She] is capable of fulfilling any major role of state".

From: *THE INDEPENDENT* Tuesday 5 September 2000

MINISTER QUITS

DRIVEN OUT

.. by a bunch of jealous, selfish, paranoid, less able and FAR less popular colleagues

I'M OFF: Mo Mowlam is driven away from Number 10 after her meeting with Tony Blair during which he agreed to let her quit the Cabinet

VOICE OF The Mirror

TRUE to form, Mo Mowlam remained loyal to the end.

She insisted that she is not quitting as an MP because she has been leaned on, let alone stabbed in the back.

Well sorry Mo, but we don't believe you.

The truth is that she's been carved up by a collection of petty political sharks.

Dumped from the Northern Ireland job, where she did so much tremendous work, Mo was brought back to a virtual non-job guaranteed to frustrate and humiliate her.

Her colleagues then began spreading poison about her mental health and ability to hold down a proper department. And her boss did nothing to stop it.

Tony Blair may not have meant to force Mo out, but that's what he did.

He should have given her a top job commensurate with her popularity and ability.

By not doing so he let Mo down, and he let the British people down.

It was an act of cowardice and betrayal and Mirror readers will be sad that she is going and furious that Mr Blair allowed it.

Mo Mowlam is open, honest, warm, loyal and committed.

So few politicians have those qualities, it is disgraceful that she should be allowed to go.

From: *THE MIRROR* Tuesday 5 September 2000

Discussion

1 *The Mirror* makes no secret of its own opinion. Are any opinions expressed in *The Independent* article? If you think there are, whose opinions are they?

2 You are not in a position to know the 'truth', you can only make your mind up from what newspapers tell you. What do you think are 'the facts' in these articles, and what are opinions?

3 What difference does the picture make to the way *The Mirror* presents its views?

Words and Spelling

1 The verbs you choose will often express your opinion.
What is the difference between 'to quit' (in *The Independent* headline) and 'driven out' (in *The Mirror* headline)?

2 What exactly is a 'whispering campaign'? Do things like that happen in a school, for example?

3 There are a number of words, especially in *The Independent* article, to do with government and politics. Make sure you know the meanings of the following, and use each one in a sentence of your own:

Parliament	general election	Cabinet Office
Minister	ministerial post	backbencher
aides		

4 There are some interesting points of spelling in the words you have just used. Notice the 'ia' digraph in the middle of 'Parliament', and the 'e' in 'aides' which makes it quite a different word from 'AIDS'.

Find out, if you haven't already, where the word 'Parliament' comes from. The biggest clue lies in the 'parli' bit at the front of the word. The word 'aides' comes from the same language.

5

> 'AIDS' is an ACRONYM. Acronyms (not to be confused with 'anagrams') are words made up of the initial letters of a group of words, which can be pronounced as a new word. Some examples are:
> NAAFI (pronounced 'naffy') = Navy, Army and Air Force Institute;
> RADA (pronounced 'rahdah') = Royal Academy of Dramatic Art;
> AIDS (pronounced 'aids') = 'acquired immunity deficiency syndrome'.
> Computer language has many acronyms. Here are some examples of common acronyms used online:
> USENET (the world's biggest bulletin board for swapping information);
> MUD (Multi-User Dungeon – a term in an interactive adventure game);
> NIMBY (Not In My Back Yard!).

Inventing acronyms can also be fun: e.g. The Worldwide Information Technology Society (TWITS or WITS?!). Write down any acronyms you already know, and invent one or two of your own. See if a friend can guess them by asking no more than twenty questions.

> **Anagrams**, in case you didn't know (although it's a word game you have probably played before), are words in which the spelling has been scrambled to make another word, e.g.
> LIFE = FILE;
> MOTHER IN LAW = WOMAN HITLER!;
> ASTRONOMERS = MOON STARERS.

6

> Notice also that 'aides' and 'AIDS' are HOMOPHONES. This means that they **sound** alike (hence the word 'phone') but are spelt differently. The English language is full of homophones, at least 600 common ones, e.g. bier/beer; bread/bred; choose/chews; great/grate; here/hear; right/write; meet/meat.

In his poem *Faithless Sally Brown* (1826), Thomas Hood wrote:

'His death, which happened in his berth,
At forty odd befell;
They went and told the sexton, and
The sexton tolld the bell' (original spelling)

Keep an eye open for some more homophones.

7 What do you think 'Downing Street insider' means? (see *The Independent* article).

8 The word 'paranoid' is used in *The Mirror* article. Find out where it comes from and what it means.

9 Look at the text under the heading, 'Voice of The Mirror'. Different styles of font have been used. Why do you think this has been done?

10 The word 'colleague' is used twice by *The Mirror*. What exactly is a 'colleague'? Notice the construction of the word and the unusual spelling at the end. Find out more about the word. Where does it come from? What other words belong to this word family?

11 The word 'commensurate' appears in 'The Voice of The Mirror'. What does it mean? Where does it come from?

12 What is a 'non-job'? Can you think of other English words that often have a 'non' in front of them? For example non-smoking.

13 What exactly is a 'dilemma'? Notice that it is spelt with double 'm' but not double 'l'. The 'di-' bit is a clue to its meaning.

Grammar and Punctuation

1 List the adjectives used by *The Mirror* to criticise or insult Mo Mowlem's colleagues. Are as many used in *The Independent*?

2 Find some adjectives used to describe Mo Mowlem. Look first in 'The Voice of The Mirror', then in *The Independent*.

3 What kind of nouns are 'cowardice' and 'betrayal'? (See 'Voice of The Mirror')

4 Compare the structure of the two headlines: 'Mowlem to quit, but the whispers continue' and 'Driven out . . . by a bunch of jealous, selfish, paranoid, less able and FAR less popular colleagues'.

   If you try to copy the structure of each headline by substituting words of your own, you will get a better idea of how they are structured, for example 'Smith to play for England, but doubts remain' or 'Egged on . . . by a crowd of noisy, angry, drunken . . .' and so on.

5 What pronouns are used in the third paragraph of 'The Voice of The Mirror' piece? Are they different from the pronouns used earlier? Why do you think there has been a change? What pronouns are used in the rest of the piece?

6 Newspapers often quote (sometimes misquote!) what people actually say. This is called verbatim reporting, which means you are using the speaker's own words. Another name for this is 'direct speech'. Find examples of verbatim reporting (or direct speech) in *The Independent* article. Are there any in *The Mirror*? Why is the caption, I'M OFF, not in inverted commas?

7 There are very noticeable differences in the layout and typography of the two texts. 'Typography' refers to the size, style and arrangement of the words printed on the page. Describe the differences.

8 There is a different style of writing in each of these articles. Which one sounds more like speech, and why?

9 Look at the pictures below. The first is from *The Independent*, the second from *The Mirror*. Look carefully at Mo Mowlem's face and the angle at which she is sitting. Are they different shots?
Now look at the more obvious difference. *The Mirror* picture has been cleverly doctored by the addition of a shadowy figure holding a knife.
What do the pictures contribute to the words of the texts? Does the open door mean anything in *The Independent* picture?

Mo Mowlam in the Cabinet Office yesterday after she announced that she would be leaving politics at the next election

from *The Independent* Tuesday 5 September 2000

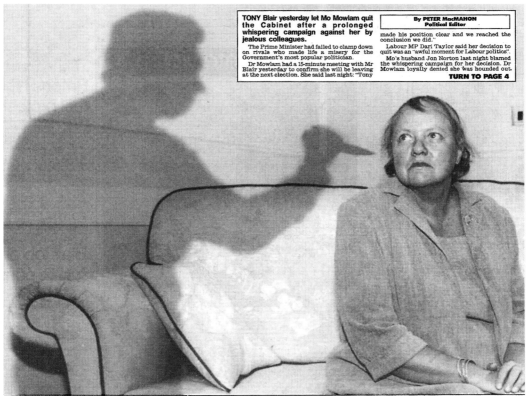

TONY Blair yesterday let Mo Mowlam quit the Cabinet after a prolonged whispering campaign against her by jealous colleagues.

The Prime Minister had failed to clamp down on rivals who made life a misery for the Government's most popular politician.

Dr Mowlam had a 15-minute meeting with Mr Blair yesterday to confirm she will be leaving at the next election. She said last night: "Tony

By PETER MacMAHON
Political Editor

made his position clear and we reached the conclusion we did."

Labour MP Dari Taylor said her decision to quit was an "awful moment for Labour politics".

Mo's husband Jon Norton last night blamed the whispering campaign for her decision. Dr Mowlam loyally denied she was hounded out.

TURN TO PAGE 4

KNIFED: Mo Mowlam after she quit yesterday. Tony Blair failed to stop his most popular Cabinet minister being stabbed in the back by a shadowy Labour whispering campaign

Your own writing

Each morning the daily newspapers serve up a breakfast of facts, but with large slices of opinion. You have to make sure what is opinion, what is fact, and try to make your own mind up.

In this unit you have looked at parts of the news devoted to Mo Mowlem by both papers. *The Mirror* even contained an exclusive article written by the politician herself, and *The Independent* even contained a short biography along with another article weighing up the pros and cons of her action.

Before you do the writing task in this unit, you will need to do some research.

Look out for a news story about a particular person. It may be a celebrity from the world of sport, TV or entertainment; it may be a politician or someone from big business; or it may be someone who has 'got into the newspapers' because of an achievement, an alleged crime or something unusual. You will then need to see if the 'story' has been covered by another newspaper, it doesn't matter which. Sometimes you may be lucky enough to get hold of two papers as the news breaks. If not, an easy way to do your research is to go to your local Reference Library and ask to see the papers for the previous week or two. Each paper will have a slightly different angle on the story – you only have to read the headlines to discover that.

When you have chosen two versions of the same story, write a report that describes the different treatment in each article. Was it front page news, for example?

To make your description thorough, you will need to look closely at each of the following:

- the headline (in the Mo Mowlem articles, for example, both headlines are statements)
- the opening paragraph
- accompanying picture(s) if any, and the captions that go with them
- the sorts of adjectives used
- the use of direct speech (verbatim reporting)
- how the paper lets its own view be known.

It will be helpful to set out your description in two columns:

	THE DAILY GIGGLE	THE MORNING GRUMBLE
HEADLINE		
OPENING PARA		
PICTURE		
ADJECTIVES		
DIRECT SPEECH		
PAPER'S OWN VIEW		

When you have finished your investigation of the two articles, write your own opinion; don't have it made for you!

UNIT TEN: *Playing Beatie Bow*

TEXT: FROM 'PLAYING BEATIE BOW', BY RUTH PARK (PENGUIN BOOKS AUSTRALIA, 1980)

Reading: Four excerpts

'Playing Beatie Bow' is a wonderful novel you will enjoy reading from start to finish, if you don't already know it. Written by Ruth Park, it is set in Sydney, Australia, in the harbour district known as The Rocks. Beatie Bow is a popular game in which young children frighten themselves silly by pretending to conjure up the ghost of a young girl called Beatie Bow, who lived in Sydney long ago. What the children in the story don't know is that the 'little furry girl' who stands and watches them but who doesn't join in, is the real ghost of Beatie Bow. The central character is Abigail, aged fourteen, who is mysteriously transported back to the time of the real Beatie Bow. Her adventures are extraordinary and sometimes horrifying.

In this unit you have four texts to read, all from the early part of the novel. The first excerpt introduces you to Abigail; the second tells you about some other children; the third describes the game of Beatie Bow; the fourth describes Abigail's journey back in time. Read all the excerpts.

1 Abigail

In the first place Abigail Kirk was not Abigail at all. She had been christened Lynette.

So for the first ten years of her life she was Lynnie Kirk, and happy as a lark. A hot-headed rag of a child, she vibrated with devotion for many things and people, including her parents. She loved her mother, but her father was a king.

So when he said goodbye to her, before he went off with another lady, she was outraged to the point of speechlessness that he could like someone so much better than herself that he didn't want to live in the same house with her any more.

'I'll come and see you often, Lynnie, I promise I shall,' he had said. And she, who could not bear to see a puppy slapped or a cockroach trodden on, hit him hard on the nose. She had never forgotten his shocked eyes above the blood-stained handkerchief. Very blue eyes they were, for he was half Norwegian.

Later she commanded her mother: 'Don't ever call me Lynnie again. Or any of those other names either'.

Kathy Kirk knew that her daughter was referring to the many pet names her father called her, for she was very dear to him.

continued

Weeks and months went past, and the person who had once been Lynette Kirk had no name at all. She would not answer to Lynette at school, and there were some puzzled notes from her teachers. Yet strangely it was through Grandmother that the ex-Lynette at last found a name.

'You'll have to do something about that hysterical little bore, Katherine,' she said. 'Just look at her, dear. She looks just like a witch with those wild eyes and her hair all in a bush.'

'You leave Lynnie alone, Mother! I've had enough of your sniping!' said Kathy in a voice in which Grandmother heard the fury and Lynette heard the shakinesss.

'Don't mind, darling,' said Kathy to ex-Lynette.
But the ex-Lynette was taken by the idea of being a witch.
'Tell me some witches' names, Mum,' she said.
'Well, there's Samantha and Tabitha,' Kathy began.
'Oh, I don't want soppy TV names,' said her daughter.
'Some real witches' names.'

'They'd have to be old ones,' said Kathy thoughtfully, 'like Hephzibah, or Susannah, or Petronella, or Abigail.'
'That's the one!' cried the girl.
'From now on I'm Abigail Kirk,' she said, 'and as soon as I'm old enough I'll change the Kirk, too.'

2 Abigail, Natalie and Vincent

Abigail jumped up with a scowl, banged the door, and went to visit the Crowns, her neighbours.

Their unit was in its customary state of theatrically awful mess. Justine Crown didn't believe in housework. She said the children came first; but she hadn't made a gold-medal job of them either. Usually Natalie, the four year old, was at kindergarten, and Vincent, the high-rise monster, at school. But as it was holidays they were both at home, and Vincent, who was in Abigail's opinion the grimmest kid two agreeable people could ever be cursed with, was at his usual game of worrying Natalie like a dog with a bone.

Natalie aroused in Abigail a solemnly protective feeling. This rather embarrassed her. The little girl was prone to sudden fevers, nightmares, fears, and had a kind of helpless affection for the frightful Vincent that did not allow her to defend herself against him.

Vincent was a bundle of bones with a puzzling smell, as though he'd wet himself six weeks earlier and not bothered to bathe. He was as sharp as a knife and had his parents sized up to the last millimetre. Abigail did not see that his face was wretched as well as cunning, and she was sincerely flattered that he hated her more than he hated everyone else.

continued

'You've got Dracula teeth,' he greeted her.

Justine shouted from the kitchen, 'Oh, for heaven's sake don't start on Abigail, you little beast.' She came out, bashing around in a basin with a fork. 'He's been dark blue hell all day.'

'Dracula teeth,' said Vincent. 'Big long white choppers. See them Fat Nat?'

'Don't call your sister that, and if Abigail's teeth are too big it's because her face hasn't grown up to them yet.'

Instantly Abigail imagined herself with this thin nosy face and fangs sticking out over her lower lip.

She was depressed with her looks as it was, and had given up hope of developing fascinating high cheekbones or eyelashes an inch long. She liked her eyebrows, which were black and straight, and her long brown hair, which glistened satisfactorily. But although her mother assured her that her figure would arrive some day, she often despaired. Most times people took her for twelve, which was humiliating.

However, she was not going to be bugged by any six-year-old dinosaur like Vincent Crown. She glared at him.

'Knock off the wisecracks!' To Justine she said, 'It's freezing outside but would you like me to take them down to the playground till it starts to get dark?'

Justine was so jubilant at the thought of being free of Natalie's unexplained tears and silences and Vincent's whining that she had the children into their anoraks and woolly caps before Abigail could think, 'Curse it, why am I such a sucker?'

3 The game

Abigail released Vincent's hard, sticky paw, and he flitted off to torment a group of fat bundles climbing on the stone wall about the playground. Let the fat bundles look after themselves, Abigail thought callously. Likely they'd have parents with them, anyway, who would pluck Vincent away from their darlings and, with any luck, half strangle him in the process.

Abigail observed the children racing dementedly back and forth but in a certain order. They were playing a group game.

'Would you like to play it, too, Natty?'

Natalie shook her head.

'They're playing Beatie Bow and it scares me. But I like to watch. Please let's watch,' pleaded Natalie.

'Never heard of it,' said Abigail. She noticed Vincent rushing to join in and thought how weird it was that in the few years that had passed since she was six or seven the kids had begun to play such different games. She watched this one just in case Vincent murdered anyone. She could already hear him squealing like a mad rat.

continued

First of all the children formed a circle. They had become very quiet. In the middle was a girl who had been chosen by some counting-out rhyme.

'That's Mudda,' explained Natalie.

'What's mudda?'

'You know, a mummy like my mummy.'

'Oh, Mother!'

'Yes, but she's called Mudda. That's in the game.'

Someone hidden behind the concrete pipes made a scraping sound. The children chorused, 'Oh Mudda, what's that?'

'Nothing at all,' chanted the girl in the centre. 'The dog at the door, the dog at the door.'

Now a bloodcurdling moan was heard from behind the pipes. Abigail felt Natalie press closer to her. She noticed that the dark was coming down fast; soon it would rain. She resolved she would take the children home as soon as she could gather up Vincent.

'Oh Mudda, what's that, what can it be?'

'The wind in the chimney, that's all, that's all.'

There was a clatter of stones being dropped. Some of the younger children squawked, and were hushed.

'Oh, Mudda, what's that, what's that, can you see?'

'It's the cow in the byre, the horse in the stall.'

Natalie held on tightly and put her hands over her eyes.

'Don't look, Abigail, it's worse than awful things on TV!'

At this point Mudda pointed dramatically beyond the circle of children. A girl covered in a white sheet or tablecloth was creeping towards them, waving and wailing.

'It's Beatie Bow,' shrieked Mudda in a voice of horror, 'risen from the dead.'

At this the circle broke and the children ran shrieking hysterically to fling themselves in a chaotic huddle of arms and legs in the sand-pit at the other end.

What on earth was all that about?' asked Abigail.

'The person who is Beatie Bow is a ghost, you see,' explained Natalie, 'and she rises from her grave, and everyone runs and pretends to be afraid. If she catches someone, that one has to be the next Beatie Bow. But mostly the children are frightened, because they play it and play it till it gets dark. Vincent gets in a state and that's why he's so mean afterwards. But the furry little girl doesn't get scared,' she added. 'I think she'd like to join in, she smiles so much. Look Abigail, see her watching over there.'

Before the older girl could look, Vincent panted up, scowling.

'We're going to play it again! I want to! I want to!'

'No way,' said Abigail firmly. 'It's getting dark and it's too cold for Natalie.'

The boy said bitterly, 'I hate you!'

'Big deal,' said Abigail.

continued

Vincent punched Natalie cruelly. Tears filled her eyes.

'You see? Just like I told you,' she said.

'What a creep you are, Vincent,' said Abigail scornfully.

Vincent made a rude gesture and ran on before them into the lobby. As they waited for the lift, Abigail saw that his whole body was trembling. She made up her mind to have a word with Justine about the too-exciting game.

'I saw the little furry girl, Vince,' said Natalie. 'She was watching you all again.'

4 Abigail goes back in time.

'Dreaming!' she thought. 'That's all. I'm dreaming.'

But the cobbles were cold and dank, her knees were stinging where she had fallen, the air was full of strange smells, horse manure and tidal flats, wood smoke, human sweat, and an all-pervading odour of sewage.

She scrambled up and ran after the child [Beatie Bow]. Strange, foreign looking women in long aprons came out of dimly lighted doorways to stare. Children, more dirty and ragged and evil looking than she had imagined children could be, looked up from floating paper boats in the gutter. One of them threw something stinking at her; it was a rabbit's head, half decayed.

She did not know where she was; all she knew was that the furry little girl might be able to tell her, so she held her skirts up to her knees and ran after her in both terror and desperation.

The furry little girl tried to lose her, ducking up dog-leg courts where the houses pressed close to the earth like lichen. Sometimes the child glanced over her shoulder as she jumped black gullies of water, or dodged urchins with hair like stiffened mop-heads. Her face was distorted with panic.

The little girl darted past the tall stone cliff of a warehouse, its huge door studded with nail-heads as if against invaders. There Abigail almost caught up with her, but a beggar with a wooden stump reared up and waved his crutch at her, shouting something out of a black, toothless mouth. And she saw that she had almost trampled on something she thought was a deformed child, until it leapt snarling to its master's crooked shoulder. It was a monkey in a hussar's uniform.

And now she had gained on the little girl, who was beginning to falter. They had turned into what Abigail did not immediately recognise as Argyle Street, though she had walked up that street a hundred times. The enormous stone arch of The Cut was different somehow. It was narrower, she thought. Where the Bradfield Highway had roared across the top of The Cut there were now two rickety wooden bridges. The houses were indescribable shanties she had never seen before, propped up with tree trunks and railway sleepers; goats grazed on their roofs; and over all was the smell of rotting seaweed, ships, wood smoke, human ordure, and horses and harness. She wondered afterwards why people had stared at her and realised that it was not because she looked strange – for with her long dress and shawl she was dressed much as they were – but because she was running.

continued

A youth with a silly face stood in her path, stroking his side whiskers and smirking, but she shoved past him. Out of a doorway bounded a grotesquely tall figure in a long white apron, brandishing what she thought was a rusty scimitar above his head. He was bellowing something like, 'Charge the heathen devils!' as he rushed past her, knocking her down as he went. She hit her head hard on the edge of the doorstep.

The pain was so sharp she was quite blinded. Other people burst from the doorway, there were cries of consternation, and she was lifted to her feet. The pain seemed to move to her ankle. She could see nothing but darkness and lights gone fuzzy and dim.

'I'm awfully sorry,' she whispered. 'I think I'm going to faint.'

You do not need to summarise these excerpts, just write down one or two details in each one that caught your imagination. It may be a bit of dialogue or a bit of description.

Discussion

1   What impressions do you get of Abigail from the four excerpts? What is she like?
    Personal names are the most important nouns in anybody's life. Why do you think losing her old name and choosing a new one were important to Abigail? Have you ever wanted to change your name?

2   What do you learn about Abigail in the second excerpt? Do you think she is tough? What do you think of Vincent? What do you think Ruth Park means when she says that Natalie 'had a kind of helpless affection for Vincent that did not allow her to defend herself against him'?
    Have you ever taken care of other people's children? How does Abigail's experience compare with yours?

3   Do you remember a children's group game that frightened you even though you enjoyed it?
    Is there any suggestion in the third excerpt that Abigail might be worried about Vincent?
    Why do you think Natalie describes the 'little girl' as 'furry'?

The third excerpt would be a good one to read out loud, with people taking different parts. Make it sound exciting.

4   What are the clues that something strange is happening to Abigail in the fourth excerpt?
    Abigail uses the word 'dreaming' but what happens to her is more like a nightmare. Which bits do you find nightmarish?

Words and Spelling

1 Everybody's name means something. There are dictionaries of names that prospective parents sometimes look at to find a name for their child – boy or girl. Find out the meanings of: Abigail, Lynette, Katherine, Samantha, Tabitha, Petronella, Natalie, Vincent, Justine, Beatrice (Beatie).

2 What do the following phrases mean?

> outraged to the point of speechlessness
> the high-rise monster
> human ordure
> all-pervading
> half decayed
> a solemnly protective feeling
> agreeable people
> prone to sudden fevers (what does 'prone' mean?)
> a hot-headed rag of a child
> dark blue hell (have you ever heard this before, or could it be Australian?)

3 There are a few insults in the second excerpt. Find them. Are any of them used today?

4 Look at the following spellings:

grotesquely	fortunately	desperation	enormous
whispered	frightened	furry	christened

Each one has a letter pattern in it that crops up very often in English words and which can also be a spelling problem.

Notice 'qu' in 'grotesquely', 'ately' in 'fortunately', 'ation' in 'desperation', 'ous' in 'enormous', 'wh' in 'whispered', 'gh' in 'frightened', 'rr' in 'furry' and 'st' in 'christened'. Choose any three of these, and list under each one as many examples as you can of the same spelling pattern. In your lists, make sure the patterns line up vertically, e.g.

grotes**qu**ely	fu**rr**y	enorm**ou**s
queue	ba**rr**icade	l**ou**se
pi**qu**e	I**rr**esponsible	ac**ou**stic

Notice especially where these spellings occur: at the beginning, in the middle, or at the end of words. Three occur at the end, for example, which is a place where many spelling errors occur. Always keep an eye on the ends of words.

Look first at 'fortunately' and compare it with 'definitely'. What do you notice? Think of three words that end in 'ately' and three that end in 'itely'. Set them out in columns making sure the suffixes line up vertically, e.g. definitely

infinitely

Grammar and Punctuation

1   Look at the third excerpt describing the game of Beatie Bow. Notice how cleverly it is put together. It is made up of three different things woven together:

a)   conversation between Abigail and Natalie (Natalie explains the game)
b)   description to tell the reader what is happening
c)   children chanting the words of the game, e.g. 'Oh, Mudda, what's that?'

Your teacher will give you a photocopy of this text, one between two. Working in pairs, one of you underline the bits where Abigail and Natalie are talking, the other put a dotted line under the bits that are spoken in the game. You could use different coloured highlighters or pencils if you wish. Make sure you agree on which bits are which before you put any marks on the paper.

The bits you are left with will be the description of what is happening. Notice that they are not written in inverted commas. If anything is, you've got something wrong somewhere.

2   Now write something along the same lines as the third excerpt. You will need to decide first of all:

a)   on a game with some speech in it
b)   on two people watching, one of whom explains the game to the other
c)   on which events to write about and how the game ends.

You don't need a mysterious 'furry girl' watching, but try to write in the vivid way that Ruth Park does.

3   Look at the following sentence from the first excerpt:

'A hot-headed rag of a child, she vibrated with devotion for many things and people, including her parents.'

What impression does it give you of Abigail?

Notice the phrase 'a hot-headed rag of a girl'. It is like other phrases often used:

A mere slip of a girl; a bit of a lad; a broth of a boy (Irish); a giant of a man; a bit of a devil.

It can also be written this way: a man of action; a woman of substance; a man of property; a time of bad luck; A Woman of no Importance (a play by Oscar Wilde); a boy of considerable intelligence; a girl of remarkable courage; a school of very high standards; a football team of left-overs and past-its.

It comes in handy now and again to make description more interesting. Ruth Park's is an original one. You think of some phrases of your own to describe someone, e.g. a long bean-pole of a boy; a rushing whirlwind of a girl.

4   Notice also, 'she vibrated with devotion'. This is another kind of phrase that is useful now and again in writing. Here are some more examples: danced with glee; shouted with exultation; talked with enthusiasm; walked with determination; smiled with satisfaction; glowered with hatred.

Write two of these in sentences of your own. If you prefer, you can use examples you have thought of.

5   There's even more to notice about the sentence 'A hot-headed rag of a child ...'. It is an interesting way of beginning a sentence because it gives you a chance to paint a picture in words about somebody or something. It is a phrase that is usually followed by a name or a pronoun. Here, it is followed by 'she' but it could have been followed by her name, 'Abigail ...'.

Look at the phrases you wrote in answer to Question 3 and write a complete sentence, using your own phrases as the first part. Here are some examples:

A mere slip of a girl, she ran rings round all of them.
A giant of a man, he soon felled all the trees.
A school of very high standards, it got good exam results.
A team of left-overs and past-its, Bugglesford Second Eleven had not won a match all season.

6   Some sentences in the excerpts above begin with an adverb or have one very near the beginning. This is an extremely useful way to start things off. Adverbs of time are particularly useful in storytelling so that readers do not lose track of what is happening. Find sentences beginning with the following:

Later ...; Now ...; Instantly ...; First of all ...; At this point ...; And now ...; She wondered afterwards ...

Choose three of these and write a pair of sentences for each, for example:

I took all day painting the fence to brighten it up. LATER I found out that I needn't have bothered; somebody had knocked it down.

7   Beatie Bow is a child from the past. Her family emigrated to New South Wales, Australia, from the Orkney Isles in Scotland. From the moment she first speaks in the story, you know straight away that she has an accent and speaks a dialect. Here are the first things she says:

'I wasna doing naething! I were only watching the bairns.'

'I dunna want it to be true.'

'Get outa the road wench! D'ye want to be run down?'

''Tis clean granny, but I'll put a touch of the comfrey paste on it, shall I?' (Abigail has grazed her knees.)

'Poor bairnie. Take a sip of granny's posset, 'tis good for you. There now, all's well . . . we'll no leave you, I promise.'

> **Accent** is a word used to describe differences in the ways people speak a language; **dialect** is a word that covers differences in vocabulary and grammar.

List examples from above where Ruth Park gives you an idea of how Beatie Bow speaks. Then list examples of dialect words and grammar.

> Dialects and accents are often called **regional** because they belong to a particular place, e.g. New Yorkers speak differently from Californians and Northern Australians speak differently from Southern Australians.

Write a short conversation between two people from your part of the country (about three speeches each) in which you use words and phonetic spelling to show the dialect and where you live. ('Phonetic spelling' means spelling a word not as it is correctly spelt, but as it sounds, as in: outa; 'tis; wasna.)

Your own writing

'Playing Beatie Bow' is a novel of 196 pages. You have looked at four brief sections of it. For the writing task in this unit, you have to imagine you are writing a novel, but don't worry, you don't have to finish it!
What you have to do is write two sketches that would appear in your novel if you ever got round to finishing it.

The first piece should be a bit like the first three excerpts you have just read. It should give readers a vivid picture of your main character and what he or she thinks about things.
The main character can be based on yourself if you wish, but must be written in the third person, NOT the first. List all sorts of things you might say about her/him (and others) before you start writing your story. Select what you want, put it in a sequence you like best, and then write. Make it seem real! Make sure there is some dialogue and lots of detail.

In the second piece, describe a mysterious going back in time. You will need to decide how it happens: following somebody? a knock on the head? a strange feeling? something odd? Again, detail will be important. Think about all the things Abigail noticed as she went back in time.

To help you there are some pictures opposite. They show the same place separated in time by one hundred years or more.

UNIT ELEVEN: *Poetry*

TEXT: PICTURE POEMS BY MICHAEL AND PETER BENTON (HODDER & STOUGHTON EDUCATIONAL, 1997).

Reading: Extracts from four poems:

1 *Look, No Hands* by U A Fanthorpe

2 *The Artist's Room* by Gillian Clarke

3 *Time, Gentle Men* by Peter Benton

4 *Child with Dove* by Gregory Harrison

Below are extracts from four poems. Read them and then look at the four pictures that follow. Each picture inspired one of the poems. Match the poems and the pictures.

1 It was hard doing this. I had to go up near the roof,
Among the girders and dusty bits. And I had to keep
On trying till I found the right place to be –
Left, and in front; not very far below her
So I could make you see how hard it is.

You have to imagine the audience. I didn't
Bother with them, they're always the same,
Ooh-ing, aah-ing, clapping, some of them
Shutting their eyes. And the smells. You have
To imagine them too; people, horses, sawdust, sweat.

You're lucky. I'm showing you what the audience
Can't really. Far off, up in the roof,

2 Where is she? Where?
Her old blue cardi's on the chair.
The window where she brushed her hair.

Her cushion, her white parasol,
the table where the sunlight fell
onto a sloping bedroom wall.

She isn't there, but this is where
She placed primroses in a jar
And gazed out at the evening star.

She stroked her cat (he's out of sight),
Took up her pen, began to write

3 It's raining civil servants, taxmen, school inspectors
Gently falling earthward in bowler hats, dark overcoats,
Clutching identical briefcases in black-gloved hands.
What do they bring I wonder? Do they feel anything?

Only the benefits of an ordered mind,
Where everything falls into place; the report is filed,
The books are balanced. The figures are agreed –
It is, very simply, an open and shut case.

Solemnly, in neat black diamonds they ascend
To meet the Chief Inspector and their promised end.
Imprinting their repeated pattern on the sky.
It is our minds the silent swarm would occupy.

4 There is a picture on our wall,
A girl in blue, a coloured ball,
A sideways-leaning gentle face,
A pigeon held in soft embrace.

I like her downward pointing toes,
The ease with which he paints her nose;
I'm just content to look and think,
I can't say what I mean in ink.

Artists:
Top left: Gwen John
Top right: Pablo Picasso
Bottom left: Edgar Degas
Bottom right: Rene Magritte

You do not need to summarise the texts this time, but write down one thing from each extract that tells you it is a poem.

Discussion

1   Look at the circus picture and the poem. What might come after 'Far off, up in the roof'? What would you have chosen to write about next?

2   The second extract ends with 'she began to write'. What do you think she might have written?

3   Think of a story that could lie behind the picture of the girl with a dove.

You are now going to look at the language of each of the poems individually.

Look, No Hands:

Words and Spelling

1   Look up the origin of these words: roof, girders, clapping, smells, horses, sawdust, sweat, lucky.
Write down alongside them, the word and the language they come from.

2   Now look at the following words: imagine, audience.
How are they built up? Where is the join?
Find as many relatives as possible to make up a word family for each of them, for example imagination, audition.

3   Look at the words 'ooh-ing' and 'aah-ing'. See if you can find 'ooh' and 'aah' in a dictionary.
The poet puts a hyphen between the first part and the 'ing'. There is no rule that says you should do this, but it seems a very sensible idea. Why do you think she did it?

Why do you think she used these words rather than 'proper' words? Do you like them?

> 'Ooh' and 'aah' could be called **phonetic spellings**. That means spelling a word to look like it sounds. There are also ONOMATOPOEIC words that sound like the sound they represent in real life, for example splash, rip, crunch, smash, murmur, tinkle, crack, cough.

One of the best places to look for onomatopoeic words is in comics and cartoons. Here are some examples:

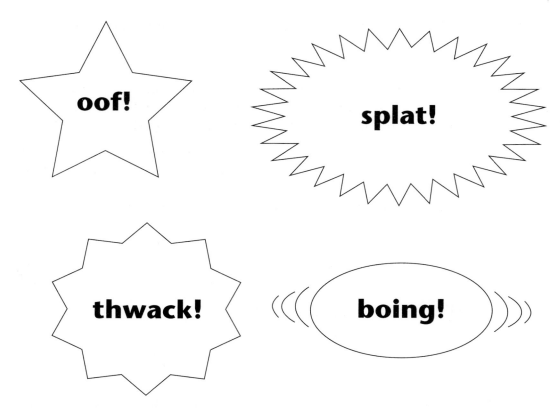

One of the unwritten rules of comic language of this kind is that the reader must recognise it as looking/sounding realistic. It can be exaggerated, but it must be convincing.

Look through some comics, and/or think of examples you know. Make a list of five or six, putting them in alphabetical order. When you have done this, imagine you have been asked to write a dictionary of these words giving, not definitions, but advice for artists on when to use them.
Here are some examples:

- Aaaaaaaaaaaaaaaaaaaaaaaaaaaagh! (somebody falling off a high building).
- Eeeeeeeeeeeeeeennnnnggggggggggooowwwwwww (a fast car going by).
- Oooof! (somebody punched in the stomach).
- Ooooooooer (sudden recognition of trouble ahead).
- Taka taka taka taka taka taka taka (machine-gun fire).

Be really imaginative. Try things like: kapow! gasplong! krrrrunch!

4 Poems tend to look narrower on the page than prose because they generally have shorter lines.
The number of syllables in a line is quite an important feature of poetry. Look at the first two verses and count the number of syllables in each line. Say them aloud in your normal voice and listen to the number of syllables you give each word. The first line for example, consists of 12 monosyllabic words and one two-syllable word ('doing'), making a total 14 syllables in

that line. Do other lines have the same number of syllables? More? Or fewer? Is there a pattern at all?

5   There are no rhymes at the ends of the lines in this poem. Rhymes create a pattern. There are however, other ways of making a pattern in poetry. Look at the first and last lines of verse one. The pattern could be called a word echo; what is it? The same thing happens in verse two; what is the echo?

6   The word 'audience' ends in a familiar suffix 'ence'. Other words end 'ance'. It is quite easy to confuse the two. Collect some examples of each and see if you can work out a way of remembering which is which. To get you started, the words listed below have a word in their family which ends in 'ence' or 'ance'. Find those words and check to see if you have spelled them correctly. Use your dictionary to search for the words. Watch out for one or two that end with a 'cy'.

appear	persist	obey	dominate
different	pretend	subside	maintain
important	radiate	insist	import
admit	enter	militant	sustain
frequent	perform	truant	violate

7   Double consonants often crop up in English spelling. There are three examples in this poem: clapping, shutting, smelly.

First, go through the alphabet to find out how many consonants in English double-up, and which ones don't. Give an example for each of those that do. Look especially at the vowel preceding the consonant.
If it is a **long vowel** as in 'hope', 'hate', 'bite', the consonant is not usually doubled: 'hoping', 'hating', 'biting'.
Now look at words in which the vowel preceding the consonant is a **short vowel** as in: 'hop', 'stop', 'rap', 'slap', 'bet', 'get', 'hit', 'cut', 'shut'. What usually happens to the consonant in words like these?

Next, go through your list of consonants that *do* double-up and try to think of English words that begin with a double consonant. Are there any at all? There are some in Welsh. Find one or two.

Now see if there are any words that end with a double consonant, and which consonants they are. Are there any long words that end with a double consonant?

Grammar and Punctuation

1   What type of sentence is the title of the poem? You can answer this by finding the verb.

2 Find examples of the first and second person pronouns in this poem. Why do you think it is written in this way?

3 Find a sentence in the poem which makes perfect sense but doesn't have a verb in it. It sounds like an exclamation.

4 In prose writing, sentences go on until they are stopped by a full stop. It doesn't matter which word comes at the end of a line, you just carry on writing. In verse, lines have to be the 'right' length for the rhythm of the poem, no matter where the full stop goes.

Look at the punctuation of this poem. Do the sentences correspond to the line lengths?
Write down an explanation of why a semi-colon and a colon have been used.

Time, Gentle Men:

Words and Spelling

1 Notice the separation of 'Gentle' and 'Men' in the title. Does it make a difference to the meaning?

2 Words go together in all sorts of ways. Apples, bananas, pears and oranges are all fruits. Sausages, pork pies, hamburgers, lamb samosas and salami are all cooked meats.
Under the headings 'tools', 'games' and 'on a car journey', list as many words as you can think of that belong to that category.

You probably found 'tools' and 'games' quite easy ones to do, rather like 'fruits' and 'cooked meats'. You probably also found that 'on a car journey' gave you a much wider choice. There are many more words that could be put in this list, but people would still guess the connection if they saw enough of them.

Here's one possible list for 'on a car journey':

route map	AA guidebook
flask of tea	luggage rack
petrol station	countryside
toilets	story tapes
hold-up	rain
motorway	café.

It's not a list like the 'fruits' and the 'games' lists, but somehow they all go together if you think of a car journey.

In the first two verses of the poem *Time, Gentle Men*, there are 64 words altogether. Quite a lot of the words go together as the words did for 'on a car journey'. The first few are: civil servants, taxmen, school inspectors, bowler hats, dark overcoats, briefcases. What do you think the others are?

What picture or ideas do these words conjure up in your mind?

3 There seem to be a lot of compound words in this poem. Compound words are two simple words joined together. There was only one in *Look, No Hands*: 'sawdust' = 'saw' + 'dust'.

In *Time, Gentle Men*, there are four compounds in the first verse alone, and if you put 'Gentle' and 'Men' back together again (Gentlemen), that makes five. There is also an interesting hyphenated word. Find them all.
There are thousands of compound words in English. Why do you think there are so many of them?

Make a list of seven compound words you can think of. Add one you have made up. See if anyone can guess which it is. Bluff your way through, when questioned. Try to convince people that it is a real word with a real meaning. You never know; it may catch on! 'Walkman', 'Greenpeace' and 'download' have all caught on in recent years.

4 Look at the word 'earthward': 'ward' is a suffix that comes from Old English and means 'moving in a particular direction'. Sometimes it is spelt, 'wards'. 'Earthward' means 'moving in the direction of earth'. See how many other words you can find, ending with 'ward'. Here is one to start with: downward.

5 Are there any rhymes in this poem?

6 Count the syllables in each line. Now read the first two verses aloud. Are there any lines with the same number of syllables?

7 Explain the following words and phrases:

● 'an ordered mind'.
● 'the books are balanced';
● 'figures are agreed';
● 'an open and shut case',

What does the last line of the poem mean?

8 The word 'civil' may strike you as odd. It doesn't just mean 'polite' in the ordinary sense. It belongs to a big family of Latin origin, which includes the words 'city' and 'civilisation'. Look the word up in a dictionary and use it in a sentence or two of your own.

Grammar and Punctuation

1 Look at the last line of the first verse and the first line of the second verse. How are they connected?

2 Are there any questions in the poem, and are they answered?

3 Look at the last line of the first verse and the last line of the poem. One contains a first person singular pronoun ('I'), the other contains a first person plural pronoun ('our'). Which line includes you?

4 There are a number of adjective/noun pairs in this poem, for example 'dark overcoats'. Occasionally, there are a couple of adjectives before the noun. Find an example of:

a) an adjective + noun
b) an adjective + adjective + noun.

5 The first verse, in fact the very first line, contains a metaphor. What is it?

The Artist's Room:

Words and Spelling

1 Why do you think the poet wrote 'cardi' and not 'cardigan'?
Think of some words you know that are often abbreviated (shortened). Write them down.
Why do people like abbreviations so much?

2 Look at the word 'parasol'. What does it mean, and where does the word come from?

3 Look at the rhyming scheme. Is it strict? What do you notice about verses one and three, compared with verse two?
What about the rhythm of the poem? You can begin to answer this question by doing some syllable counting. How many syllables in each line? Is there any variation?

4 Notice the word 'cushion'. It ends with the suffix 'ion'. Think of as many words as you can, ending in 'ion'. Notice how a 'sh' sound often comes before 'ion' but look at how many different ways the 'sh' sound is spelt. For example, there is 'cushion', 'passion' and 'condition'. Sort the words you have found into groups, according to their spelling of the 'sh' sound.

Grammar and Punctuation

1 What kind of a sentence does the poem begin with? Who do you think is speaking it?

2 The two poems you have looked at earlier began each line with a capital letter. Check to remind yourself. Many poems are written in this way. Capital letters normally start new sentences, but in poems they can mark the start of a new line. It's a 'rule' many poets observe, but not all.

Look now at *The Artist's Room* and look particularly at where the full stops are placed. Now look at the beginnings of the lines. What 'rule' does the poet

Gillian Clarke follow when it comes to capital letters? The answer to a question about beginnings lies, oddly enough, in the full stops at the ends.

3 More about sentences:

- How many are there in the first verse?
- What do you notice about the second verse? Is it a sentence?
- How many verbs are there in the third verse which consist of only one sentence? (Watch out for 'to be' verbs.)
- How many verbs are there in the fourth part? (Again, watch out for the 'to be' verb and the cat!)

4 The bit about the cat is placed in **parentheses**, between commas as well as brackets. Why do you think the poet used parentheses?

Write two sentences of your own in which you use parentheses to include a bit of incidental or extra information.

Child With Dove:

Words and Spelling

1 This poem is written in what are called 'rhyming couplets'. What do you think they are?

2 Are the words that sound alike, spelt alike?

3 It is also written in octosyllabic lines. Phew! What on earth are they?! Well, work it out. You know what a syllable is; find out what 'octo' means. Then do some counting.

4 There are two hyphenated words in the poem: 'sideways-leaning' and 'downward-pointing'. Both are about direction. Notice also the suffix 'ward' which cropped up in *Time, Gentle Men*.
It is quite a clever way of saying exactly what you want to say in the fewest words.
Write three sentences of your own using a hyphenated word to describe something. You are allowed to invent them, for example a metal-eating monster; goal-crazy fans; dog-walking pensioners in the park.

5 In the first verse, what do you notice about the way three of the lines begin? Why do you think they begin this way?

Try this idea for yourself. First choose one of the following that takes your fancy:

> There is a picture in my room,
> or
> There is a photo on my desk,
> or
> I like this painting of a zoo,
> or
> Some funny creatures then appeared,

Here is a recipe to help you write your own verse:

> Take one first line from above.
> Write another octosyllabic line that rhymes with it.
> Make sure your line begins with 'A . . .' (the indefinite article)
> Now write a third and fourth line.
> Make sure they are octosyllabic.
> Make sure they rhyme.
> Make sure they begin with an 'A'.
> Watch out for the commas!
> When completed, read it out to a friend. You could even illustrate it and display it.

Grammar and Punctuation

1 Which pronoun tells you that the pcet isn't just talking about himself, and which one tells you he is?

2 Where in the poem is there a list?

3 There is quite a bit of description in this poem. Find three nouns that have one or more adjectives in front of them. Now find a noun where the descriptive word comes after it. A good clue is the word 'in'.

Your own writing

1 Before writing anything, read the complete versions of the four poems you have been studying. Your teacher will give them to you. If you read them aloud, you will enjoy them even more, and understand them better.

2 When you come to do GCSE English you will be expected to write about poems you have read and what you think about them. To do this you will need to know something about poetry as well as knowing what you think about a poem. This means looking closely at what poets do with language.

There are lots of things that poets do with language that are exactly the same as everybody else's uses of language. For example, they use lots of ordinary words. They also ask questions, make statements, give commands and even exclaim.

● Make a list of the things poets do with language that are the same as other people's uses of language.

Poets also do different things with language. They *do* use ordinary words, but they tend to choose them very carefully.
One of the first things you have probably noticed is that the poems you have just studied look quite different on the page from any other text in this book. They are very narrow and use short lines! How neat they look!
You will also have noticed that there is a different rhythm or 'feel' to language in poems.

● Now make a list of things you have noticed that make poems different from the other texts in this book.

When you have made your list, find an example for each point. If you have said that lines do not always rhyme, give an example. If you have said that they do rhyme sometimes, give an example.

Remember to make sure you mention all the four poems that you have studied.

Your first paragraph could be about ordinary things poets do with language, and your second paragraph could be about unusual and clever things they do.
For your third paragraph, write about the poem you like best out of the four. Say what you like about it, and what the poet has done to make the poem enjoyable.

Make the title of your writing a question: WHAT DO POETS DO WITH LANGUAGE?

Here is the plan again, to remind you:

● A **first paragraph** on ordinary things poets do with language.
● A **second paragraph** on unusual and clever things they do with language.
● A **third paragraph** telling the reader about a poem you enjoyed and why.

UNIT TWELVE: *Newspapers (Part Two)*

TEXTS: CONCORDE FLIGHT 4590: NEWS ACCOUNTS OF THE PRELIMINARY ACCIDENT REPORT (2 SEPTEMBER 2000)

Reading

Overleaf is a news account of the preliminary report on the Air France Concorde crash in July, 2000. It comes from *The Mirror*, published on 2 September, 2000. Read it and summarise the main information in one or two sentences.

Discussion

1   The preliminary report on the crash caused many aviation experts to doubt that Concorde would ever fly again. What is/was so special about this plane?

2   The article gives the reader some important information, but there are two statements about the fire drill that don't add up. Which are they, and what is it that doesn't quite make sense?

3   Another newspaper on the same day, reported that the piece of tyre rubber found on the runway weighed 8.8 pounds (4kg) and that the piece of metal was 13 inches long (32.5cms approx). The other paper also gives a take-off time of 14.42 and 21 seconds, whereas *The Mirror* gives the time of take-off as 4.42pm. How important do you think it is to report factual details accurately?

Words and Spelling

1   The name of the plane, Concorde, is French in origin, and with the final 'e', French in spelling. If you have been to Paris, you may have visited Place de la Concorde. When used as an ordinary word in English, it is spelt without the final 'e' and with a lower case 'c': concord.
Find out what it means, and why the word should have been used to name this particular plane.

2   In the article there are a number of words and phrases that denote uncertainty about something. Find some examples and say why they have to be used.
Exactly what are the facts in this article? List them.

3   How often is the report referred to? Is any other report mentioned?

THIS WASN'T SWEPT UP AND CONCORDE CRASHED

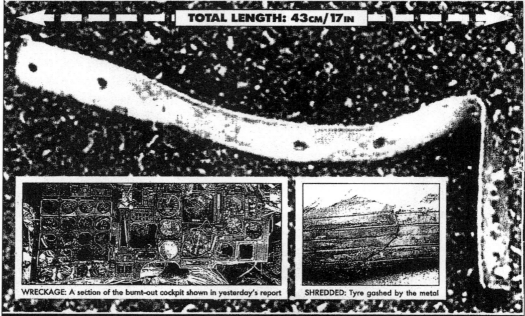

TOTAL LENGTH: 43cm/17in

WRECKAGE: A section of the burnt-out cockpit shown in yesterday's report

SHREDDED: Tyre gashed by the metal

KEY TO TRAGEDY: The suspect metal strip, confirmed yesterday as the trigger for the chain of events that caused Concorde to crash in flames

Metal on runway sparked disaster

By MARK DOWDNEY
Foreign Editor

THIS is the piece of twisted metal that downed Concorde, pinpointed yesterday in the preliminary report on the disaster.

The 43-centimetre strip, believed to have fallen off another plane, was found on the runway after the July 25 crash which killed 113 people.

It burst a tyre on the Air France Concorde, sending chunks of rubber smashing into a wing fuel tank and sparking the fatal blaze.

The runway at Paris's Charles de Gaulle airport had not been properly inspected for 12 hours before the supersonic airliner took off at 4.42pm. An inspection due at 3pm was postponed because of a fire drill.

No one spotted the metal – with tragic consequences.

Presenting the report, Paul-Louis Arslanian, head of France's Air Accident Investigation Bureau (BEA), said staff normally inspected the runway three times a day.

The first inspection on July 25 was at 4.30am.

The western side was checked briefly at noon after a plane was believed to have hit a bird. The next full inspection was due at 3pm.

Debris from Concorde, including a piece of burning tyre weighing over 9lb, was found on the runway after the crash.

Investigators also discovered more than 12 pieces of metal that did not come from the crash jet.

Among these was the metal strip, bent into an L-shape, which burst the tyre.

The plane was going too fast to stop its take-off.

Less than two minutes later the crippled jet plunged in flames into a small hotel, killing all 109 on board and four people on the ground.

Later, the metal strip was found to match a gash in the tyre. The BEA report says the source of the metal is not yet known.

It is pierced with a number of holes, contains rivets used on aircraft and is covered in a material used to coat plane surfaces.

No airline which used the runway the

day before Concorde crashed reported any missing parts on its aircraft, said the report.

Some jets have been inspected by crash investigators.

"I am confident that if someone finds out it fell off his plane, he will not conceal it." Mr Arslanian said. A BEA spokesman said: "We think it is from another aircraft, but further analysis is necessary to be sure."

Mr Arslanian cautioned against drawing hasty conclusions about the postponed fire drill. "We have not looked at the issue of runway inspections yet," he said.

"It's too early in the process. We need to understand what was done in the fire drill."

He added that no aircraft which used the runway before Concorde reported any problems. The final report into the crash is not expected for at least a year.

The BEA boss would not say when the grounded Concordes might be cleared to fly again.

m.dowdney@mgn.co.uk

from *THE MIRROR* Saturday 2 September 2000

4   Find the word 'postponed'. How is it constructed? Where do you think the join is? Look up the word. The prefix 'post' is a clue to its origin. You will also find that 'post' is a word in its own right, and that it has a number of meanings. Concentrate for now on 'post' as a prefix, and write down seven words that use this prefix. Check that you know how to spell them.
    What does the prefix 'post' mean, and how is it connected to your 'posterior'?!

5   Some other words to note are: pierce; wreckage; analysis; bureau; confirmed; necessary. Find one other word for each that is spelt in a similar way, for example wreckage/wrapping.
    'Necessary' is a word often misspelt and it is difficult to think of a word similar to it. Some people remember how to spell it by saying to themselves 'a shirt has one collar (one 'c') and two sleeves (two 's's)'. It might sound a bit daft, but it always works.

> Tricks to help you remember a number or a spelling are called
> **mnemonics**, a Greek word that is a spelling headache in its own right!

6   Notice the use of the word 'key' as a metaphor (see Unit Six). Explain how the word 'sparked' in the sub-heading, is both literally true and also a metaphor. Use the metaphor 'sparked off' in three sentences of your own.

7   Are there any other metaphors in this article?

8   In this text there are also a number of words to do with investigation. List them.

Grammar and Punctuation

1   Look at the headline over the picture. Notice two words in particular: 'This' and the word 'and'. Would you know what the word 'this' referred to, if there were no picture?
    Now look at the conjunction 'and'. It connects two statements: 'This wasn't swept up' is the first one, while the second is 'Concorde crashed'. It does not actually say that Concorde crashed *because* the piece of metal wasn't swept up, but it IMPLIES that. It implies a cause and an effect.

> IMPLYING means you are suggesting a meaning but not actually saying it.
> Other words in this family are: implication; imply; implicit; implied;
> implicitly and implicated. Look them all up.

To get at implied meanings you have to read between the lines, as people say.

Look at the following statements connected by 'and', and say what the implied meaning is:

> **a)** This bike is the latest model and it is the best.
> **b)** This cream contains special ingredients and it clears up spots.
> **c)** The teacher told them all off and they won the attendance trophy.
> **d)** She didn't do what I said and she lost the match.
> **e)** He did his homework and passed the exam.

Did you notice that the implied word is 'because'? Now turn all the sentences back to front and connect each half with a 'because'. The first one has been done for you:

a) It is the best BECAUSE this bike is the latest model. (Newest is best!)

Now do the other four. Notice how the meaning is not implicit now but EXPLICIT. In speech, you can use 'and' to mean 'because' and people have a way of knowing what you mean. A lot of what we say in speech is implicit, and that is perfectly all right. It's natural. In writing however, there is a need to be explicit, to be more exact, because you and your friendly face won't be there when somebody reads it.

The Mirror article is a piece of writing though, so why have they used 'and' in this way? Could it be because they like their headlines to sound as much as possible like everyday speech?

Before discussing this question with a partner, here is another piece of information for you to think about. The preliminary report actually said that the piece of metal 'almost certainly' gashed Concorde's tyre. Does this throw any light on matters?

2 Using 'and' as a connector for just about everything sometimes has a comical effect. Here are some examples:

> **a)** Our dog eats anything and is especially fond of children.
> **b)** Granny had all her teeth out last year and a new gas oven put in.
> **c)** I put the kettle on and the roof fell in.

Rewrite them to remove the misunderstanding.

3 Find the following three verbs in the Concorde article: 'downed', 'pinpointed' and 'sparked'. Two of them come from words that are usually used as nouns, the third comes from a word usually used as an adverb. Which are which?

4 Find four adverbs that have been used in this text and say why they have been used. Remember, adverbs usually mean you are being careful about what you say, or enthusiastic. To help you: three of them are 'ly' adverbs and another one, used twice, begins with a 't'.

5 There is only one modal verb in this text. What is it? Where is it? And why has it been used?

6 Look at the following sentence:

> The runway at Paris's Charles de Gaulle airport had not been properly inspected for 12 hours before the supersonic airliner took off.

Look at the verb in the middle of it: 'had not been . . . inspected'. Notice that the subject of the sentence (the runway) didn't do the verb, somebody else did it (or didn't do it in this case!). Runways can hardly inspect themselves.

> When a verb is used in this way it is called the **passive voice**. Don't worry about the word 'voice', all it means here is a particular way of expressing yourself. It is an **impersonal** way because it doesn't tell you who did or didn't do the verb. Its opposite, and the voice we use most frequently, is the **active voice**. This is more **personal** because you know exactly who did or didn't do it. Here are some examples.

ACTIVE VOICE	PASSIVE VOICE
I threw the ball.	The ball was thrown.
Mrs Smith filled the big basin to the brim.	The big basin was filled to the brim.
Jack has smashed the window.	The window has been smashed.
She made it happen.	It just happened.
Has Dr Jones examined you?	Have you been examined?
The inspectors detected a green gas.	A green gas was detected.
They saw him sneak into the cinema.	He was seen to sneak into the cinema.
The mechanics were overhauling it.	It was being overhauled.

In the first column you know exactly who did the throwing, the filling, the making, the examining, the detecting and the sneaking. In the second column you are told these things were done, but not by whom.

Notice too that words like 'was', 'has been' and 'being' are used to make verbs passive.

Another way of understanding the difference between active and passive is to say:
if I, you, he, she, they and it *did* the verb then it is **active**, but if we all had it *done to us*, it is **passive**.

The passive is useful for two things:

a) It enables you to be objective in report writing, especially technical or legal reports.

b) It enables you to get out of trouble (you hope!) e.g.

Teacher: Why are these on the floor?
Pupil: They've been knocked over, Miss.
Teacher: But who did it?
Pupil: Dunno, Miss. It just happened.

Now refer back to the newspaper report.

Paragraph ten contains a verb in the active voice: 'Investigators also discovered . . .'. Elsewhere in the text there are at least five uses of the passive voice. Find and list three examples of the active voice and three examples of the passive. Discuss your lists with your teacher.

7 The word 'suspect' is used at the bottom of the picture. Like so many English words, it can be used as a noun, a verb or an adjective. How is it being used here? What other words belong to this word family?

8 Note the contraction in the headline ('wasn't'). Why do you think they put this, rather than 'was not'?

9 Adjectives can add an emotional or dramatic touch to the nouns they describe. Find three adjective/noun pairs in this text that you think are expressive.

10 Are there any examples of verbatim reporting (direct speech) in this text? Why do you think these particular bits have been quoted?

11 There are four colons altogether in this text. Find them, and say why each one has been used.

12 Why has the dash been used after the word 'metal'? (see second column).

13 Look at the two headlines and the first paragraph of the text. What do you notice about what they are saying?

Now look at another newspaper article (on page 97) published in *The Guardian* on the same day. When you have read it, do the activities on the following page.

Final 77 seconds of crashed Concorde

Jon Henley in Paris

The final terrifying moments of Air France flight 4590 were revealed yesterday as French accident investigators released their preliminary report on last month's Concorde crash outside Paris that killed 113 people.

In a chilling transcript, the cockpit voice recorder graphically describes the final 77 seconds as the pilot, Christian Marty, struggles for control of the airliner, by now shooting flames from its left wing.

At 2.43pm, shortly after take-off, the control tower warned: "Concorde zero ... 4590, you have flames. You have flames behind you."

The crew, unable to retract the undercarriage and losing power fast, tried desperately to reach nearby Le Bourget airport. Seven seconds after the first message from air traffic control, the chief navigator confirmed: "Breakdown engine two." Then, four seconds later: "Cut engine two."

As the aircraft tried to gain speed for an emergency landing, Mr Marty, in his last words, was heard to say: "Too late ... No time." Just after 2.44pm, the co-pilot exclaimed: "Le Bourget, Le Bourget. Negative; we are trying Le Bourget." Sixteen seconds later, the recording ends. The plane ploughed into a hotel in the small town of Gonesse.

The crash prompted Air France to ground its remaining Concordes immediately; British Airways followed suit three weeks later.

The investigators from the French accident inquiry board, BEA, confirmed their earlier hypothesis that a burst tyre had set off the fatal chain of events that downed the New York-bound plane, killing all those on board – mainly German passengers and nine crew – and four people on the ground.

"The July 25 accident shows that the destruction of a tyre, an event that we cannot say will not recur, had catastrophic consequences ... preventing the crew from rectifying the situation," the report said. "The crew had no way of knowing about the nature of the fire, nor any means of fighting it."

It confirmed that a metal strip, probably from another plane, had been found on the runway. "It has holes in it and in some of these holes appear to be Cherry aeronautical rivets. This strip has not been identified as coming from Concorde," the report said.

The BEA said last month that the 16-inch piece of metal had "almost certainly" gashed the Concorde's tyre, sending large chunks of rubber hurtling at tremendous speed into the plane's fuel tanks, contained in its delta-shaped wings, and sparking the blaze.

"At least one fuel tank was ruptured in one or more places, resulting in a substantial fuel leak. The leaking fuel caught light and a very violent fire ensued throughout the duration of the flight. Engine problems occurred in engine number two and, briefly, in engine number one," yesterday's interim report, released on the internet, said.

Over the 25 years Concorde has been in commercial operation, there have been at least seven incidents in which one or more of the plane's tyres have burst, leading to punctures in the wings or fuel tanks.

But in all of those incidents it was a piece of flying metal – from the undercarriage or water deflectors – that caused the damage, not tyre rubber itself. Safety efforts were therefore concentrated on strengthening all metal parts that could be broken off in a tyre burst, but not on protecting the wings.

from *THE GUARDIAN* Saturday 2 September 2000

1   Search for information (facts) that appear in both articles. List them briefly. Also, make a note of any words or phrases that occur in both texts.

2   List information in *The Guardian* that does not appear in *The Mirror*.

3   List information in *The Mirror* that does not appear in *The Guardian*.

4   Work out the average sentence length for each article. Is there much difference?

5   Apart from the fact that one article is a bit longer, what do you think are the main differences between the two articles?

6   Some paragraphs in *The Guardian* article consist of only one, very long sentence. Find two examples of this.

7   Find a paragraph consisting of more than one sentence in *The Guardian* article.

8   Why has 'almost certainly' been written in inverted commas? Compare the use of the adverb 'almost' with the first and third paragraphs of *The Mirror* article. What difference does the 'almost' make?

9   What is a transcript? (See second paragraph). Why has it been described as 'chilling'?

 # Your own writing

With the two articles combined you have quite a lot of information about a terrible disaster (about 1150 words altogether). Your task is to tell the story of the Concorde crash for a pictorial history book covering events in the early years of the 21st century. The publishers have allowed no more than 200 words, so be selective in what you say. Don't just concentrate on the piece of metal, use other information to cover the whole of the event. Only write about information contained in the articles. Think of a suitable title for your account.

UNIT THIRTEEN: *Texts Online*

TEXT: BBC WEBSITE: THE REALLY WILD ZONE (www.bbc.co.uk/reallywild)

Reading

Read the following text printed from 'The Really Wild Zone' on the BBC Nature website. What you cannot see, of course, are the moving images, the colour and the various kinds of highlighting, e.g. words flashing on and off. Neither do you have a cursor to give you control over the text displayed.

Discussion

1 Why do you think nature has been such a popular topic for so long on TV? Think of David Attenborough's programmes, for example.

2 Think of two or three things that make reading a website page different from reading a page in most nature books published in the last hundred years. Discuss advantages and disadvantages of IT texts. You can draw on your own experience of using the Internet and of reading nature books.

3 The BBC clearly thinks that 'really' is an important part of the page's title, 'The Really Wild Zone'. It is used a great deal nowadays, for example 'The really useful guide to playing the guitar'. A similar word is 'seriously': 'seriously fit'; 'I'm seriously into this'; 'The seriously good cookbook'. Why do you think we use these adverbs such a lot?

Words and Spelling

1 How would you spell the plural of 'hippo'? Have a go and then check the dictionary.
You probably know that 'hippo' is short for a longer word. Can you spell the longer word? Have a go.
The longer word, in its plural form, can be spelt two ways. Find out what they are.

There are some other Latin words used in English that end in 'us': syllabus, omnibus, radius, rhombus.
Check their meanings if you are not sure and look up the spellings of the plural forms. Are there any that can be spelt in a different way? If so, which way do you prefer?

2 The verb 'secrete' is used in the 'did you know?' box. It has two meanings: one is connected with the word 'secret', the other with the word 'excrete'. Find out which meaning is used here.

3 A shortened word like 'hippo' is regarded as an informal use of language. Find some more informal words in this text. Here is one to start you off: 'kids'. If you have ever wondered how parents and teachers came to call you all kids, you can blame the Vikings for it!

4 Notice the phrase 'Fun Stuff' in the left-hand column. 'Stuff' and 'thing' are very useful, all-purpose nouns that can mean anything you like. They work best in speech, for example 'What's all that stuff?,' 'Get that thing out of here'. They can be just informal or downright insulting, especially if used to refer to your personal belongings. There is however, a brand of hand-cleaning gel specially made to wash off oil and dirt, called 'That Stuff'. 'Wash it off with some of that stuff.'

Often the two words are used to cover up the fact that you don't know what something is actually called: 'You pull that thing don't you, to get it going?' Other versions are: thingummy, thingamabob, thingamajig, thingy, how's your father, doodah. You can use them in speech when you want to be informal, but remember that the nurse won't find it very helpful if all you can tell her is that you trapped your thingummy in the doodah on the how's your father! If you use them in writing, make sure you know why, for example to sound friendly on a website page.

5   Notice how conveniently the word 'drey' rhymes with 'grey'. Find out what a 'drey' is. The word 'squirrel' means 'shadow tail'. Find out where it comes from. If you ever feel you would like to write a short story about a cheeky squirrel who wreaks havoc in your garden but is never caught, don't you think Shadowtail would make a good title?

6   Notice the word 'priorities' in the left-hand column. You can guess what many things are in that list, but 'priorities' is just a bit puzzling. Find out what the word means. To find out what the BBC means by it in this web page you would have to search under that heading.

Make a list of the seven priorities in your life. Seven is a lucky number!

Note how the singular form of the word (priority) is spelt with a 'y' at the end. Think of three other words where the plural spelling converts 'y' into 'ies'.

7   When this book was being written, nobody could find 'animorph' in the dictionary. Do you think it could be a word invented by the writer of the web page? In the world of computer games new words are frequently being invented, but this one couldn't be found even in a 1997 computer dictionary. Guess what it could mean, and see if you can find out. There are for example, some exciting stories about creatures called animorphs by K.A. Applegate in *The Invasion, The Encounter,* and *The Visitor*, (Scholastic).

8   Among the different kinds of words in this text are two technical terms: 'carnivores' and 'predators'. What do they mean? Why has the adjective 'fearsome' been used?

9   Note the 'cyclo' in 'Encyclopedia'. Why do you think it is there? Note also that the word can be spelt in two ways: 'encyclopedia' and 'encyclopaedia'. You will even find 'cyclopedia' in the dictionary.

10 See if you can find the acronym in this text.

Grammar and Punctuation

1   How many questions is the reader asked in this text? What is missing from the last question?

2   How many sentences are there telling you to do something? (Imperatives or commands.)

3 There is only one statement in this text. Which is it? Remember that it will have to contain a verb.

4 A great many of the words in this text are titles or labels. Why should this be so?

5 There are eight compound nouns in this text altogether. One has been used twice; three others have a plural ending. Find them.

6 There is one modal verb in this text. Find it and say why it has been used.

7 A first person plural pronoun has been used once. Find it. Why has it been used?

8 What do you think 'my BBC' could refer to?

9 Notice the verb 'Check out' under 'Carnivores'. Many English verbs have a preposition added to them. Each preposition creates a different meaning. What does 'Check out' mean in this text? What other meaning can 'check out' have? What are the different meanings of the following: check in; check off; check over; check through.

10 The verb 'get' is used twice. It is a much used verb in speech. Some people don't like it very much, but it is almost impossible not to use it. Not only that, it is joined to a number of prepositions to give it an amazingly wide range of meanings. Put the following into sentences to show what they mean. Imagine you are writing sentences in a guide book for people learning English.

get off with	get on with	get over it	get away
you'll get by	get off	get on with it	get through
get with it	get after him	get in	get out
get up	get down to it	get out and get under	get behind

If you think some of these have two meanings (e.g. 'get up' can mean 'get out of bed' or 'get off the floor'), write two sentences to show the difference.

Apart from the ones above, there are lots of other well known phrases that use the verb 'get':

Get lost; get real; get stuffed; get knotted; get a life; get away with you; get sorted; get organised.

They all seem to be insults or criticisms. Do you agree? Can you think of a pleasant use of the word 'get'?

11 This text is an interactive text. What does that mean? What is there in the language that makes it interactive?

12 Language is used to do jobs, for example ask questions, tell people what to do. How many different jobs does the language in this text do? List them.

13 What is the purpose of the 'did you know?' box?

14 How is the text organised on the page? How many different sections are there? What kinds of things are in each of the sections?

Your own writing

Your writing task in this unit is to write an opening page for a website of your own on absolutely any subject you like. It will need to be an interactive text, quite different from other texts you have written in these units.

You will need to brainstorm the subject first and then arrange it on a website page so that your readers can find their way around easily. You will need to arrange your information and messages in different sections, and you will need labels or headings for different topics. You can have a 'did you know?' box if you wish, together with your own logos and graphics. Make the page attractive, interesting and useful.

UNIT FOURTEEN: *A Korean Folk-Tale*

TEXT: FROM *CLASSIC FOLK-TALES FROM AROUND THE WORLD*

 Reading: *Pigling and her Proud Sister*

PIGLING AND HER PROUD SISTER — A KOREAN FOLK-TALE

PEAR BLOSSOM had been the name of a little Korean maid who was suddenly left motherless. When her father, Kang Wa, who was a magistrate high in office, married again, he took for his wife a proud widow whose daughter, born to Kang Wa, was named Violet. Mother and daughter hated housework and made Pear Blossom clean the rice, cook the food and attend to the fire in the kitchen. They were hateful in their treatment of Pear Blossom, and, besides never speaking a kind word, called her Pigling, or Little Pig, which made the girl weep often. It did no good to complain to her father, for he was always busy. He smoked his yard-long pipe and played checkers hour by hour, apparently caring more about having his great white coat properly starched and lustred than for his daughter to be happy. His linen had to be beaten with a laundry club until it glistened like hoar frost, and, except his wide-brimmed black horsehair hat, he looked immaculately white when he went out of the house to the Government office.

Poor Pigling had to perform this task of washing, starching, and glossing, in addition to the kitchen work, and the rat-tat-tat of her laundry stick was often heard in the outer room till after midnight, when her heartless stepsister and mother had long been asleep.

There was to be a great festival in the city, and for many days preparations were made in the house to get the father ready in his best robe and hat, and the women in their finery, to go out and see the king and the royal procession.

Poor Pigling wanted very much to have a look at the pageant, but the cruel stepmother, setting before her a huge straw bag of unhulled rice and a big cracked water jar, told her she must husk all the rice, and, drawing water from the well, fill the crock to the brim before she dared to go out on the street.

What a task to hull with her fingers three bushels of rice and fill up a leaky vessel! Pigling wept bitterly. How could it ever be done?

While she was brooding thus and opening the straw bag to begin spreading the rice out on mats, she heard a whir and a rush of wings and down came a flock of pigeons. They first lighted on her head and shoulders,

continued

and then hopping to the floor began diligently, with beak and claw, and in a few minutes the rice lay in a heap, clean, white, and glistening, while with their pink toes they pulled away the hulls and put these in a separate pile.

Then, after a great chattering and cooing, the flock was off and away. Pigling was so amazed at this wonderful work of the birds that she scarcely knew how to be thankful enough. But, alas, there was still the cracked crock to be filled. Just as she took hold of the bucket to begin there crawled out of the fire hole a sooty black imp, named Tokgabi.

"Don't cry," he squeaked out. "I'll mend the broken part and fill the big jar for you." Forthwith, he stopped up the crack with clay, and pouring a dozen buckets of water from the well into the crock, it was filled to brimming and the water spilled over on all sides. Then Tokgabi the imp bowed and crawled into the flues again, before the astonished girl could thank her helper.

So Pigling had time to dress in her plain but clean clothes that were snow-white. She went off and saw the royal banners and the king's grand procession of thousands of loyal men.

The next time, the stepmother and her favourite daughter planned a picnic on the mountain. So the refreshments were prepared and Pigling had to work hard in starching the dresses to be worn – jackets, long skirts, belts, sashes, and what not, until she nearly dropped with fatigue. Yet instead of thanking and cheering her, the cruel stepmother told Pigling she must not go out until she hoed all the weeds out of the garden and pulled up all the grass between the stones of the walk.

Again the poor girl's face was wet with tears. She was left at home alone, while the others went off in fine clothes, with plenty to eat and drink, for a day of merrymaking.

While weeping thus, a huge black cow came along and out of its great liquid eyes seemed to beam compassion upon the kitchen slave. Then, in ten mouthfuls, the animal ate up the weeds, and, between its hoof and lips, soon made an end of the grass in the stone pathway.

With her tears dried, Pigling followed this wonderful brute out over the meadows into the woods, where she found the most delicious fruit her eyes ever rested upon. She tasted and enjoyed, feasting to the full, and then returned home.

When the jealous stepsister heard of the astonishing doings of the black cow, she determined to enjoy a feast in the forest also. So on the next gala-day she stayed home and let the kitchen drudge go to see the royal parade. Pigling could not understand why she was excused, even for a few hours, from the pots and kettles, but she was still more surprised by the gift from her stepmother of a rope of cash to spend for dainties. Gratefully thanking the woman, she put on her best clothes and was soon on the main street of the city enjoying the gay sights and looking at the happy people. There were tight-rope dancing, music with drum and flute by bands of strolling players, tricks by conjurers and mountebanks, with mimicking and castanets, posturing by the singing girls and fun of all sorts. Boys

continued

peddling honey candy, barley sugar, and sweetmeats were out by the dozen. At the eating-house, Pigling had a good dinner of fried fish, boiled rice with red peppers, turnips, dried persimmons, roasted chestnuts and candied orange, and felt as happy as a queen.

The selfish stepsister had stayed home, not to relieve Pigling of work, but to see the wonderful cow. So, when the black animal appeared and found its friend gone and with nothing to do, it went off into the forest.

The stepsister at once followed in the tracks of the cow but the animal took it into its head to go very fast, and into unpleasant places. Soon the girl found herself in a swamp, wet, miry, and full of brambles. Still hoping for wonderful fruit, she kept on until she was tired out and the cow was no longer to be seen. Then, muddy and bedraggled, she tried to go back, but the thorny bushes tore her clothes, spoiled her hands, and so scratched her face that when at last, nearly dead, she got home, she was in rags and her beauty was gone.

But Pigling, rosy and round, looked so lovely that a young man from the south, of good family and at that time visiting the capital, was struck with her beauty. And as he wanted a wife, he immediately sought to find out where she lived. Then he secured a go-between who visited both families and made all the arrangements for the betrothal and marriage. Grand was the wedding. The groom, Su-wen, was dressed in white and black silk robes, with a rich horsehair cap and head-dress denoting his rank as a Yang-ban, or gentleman. On his breast, crossed by a silver-studded girdle, was a golden square embroidered with flying cranes rising above the waves—the symbols of civil office. He was tall, handsome, richly cultured, and quite famous as a writer of verses, besides being well read in the classics.

Charming, indeed, looked Pear Blossom, as she was now called again, in her robe of brocade, and long undersleeves which extended from her inner dress of snow-white silk. Dainty were her red kid shoes curved upward at the toe. With a baldric of open-worked silver, a high-waisted long skirt, with several linings of her inner silk robes showing prettily at the neck, and the silver bridal ring on her finger, she looked as lovely as a princess.

Besides her bridal dower, her father asked Pear Blossom what she preferred as a special present. When she told him, he laughed heartily. Nevertheless he fulfilled her wishes and to this day, in the boudoir of Pear Blossom, now Mrs. Su-wen, there stands an earthen figure of a black cow moulded and baked from the clay of her home province, while the pigeons like to hover about a pear tree that bursts into bloom every spring-time and sheds on the ground a snowy shower of fragrant petals.

Discussion

1   Lots of fairy stories and folk-tales have similar plots and events in them. Does this old tale from Korea remind you of any other stories you know?

2   A modern Korean student's interpretation of this story is: never give up, you might get lucky! What do you think is the meaning or the moral of this tale? Do you think 'proud' is the right adjective to describe Violet?

3   If not exactly bullied, Pear Blossom has been victimised by her step relatives. Why do you think people victimise other people? Or, put it another way, how do people become victims?

Words and Spelling

1   Notice that the suffix 'ling' has been added to the word 'pig', when in English normally, the word would be 'piglet', meaning 'a little pig' but also used affectionately about humans. Why do you think the translator has used the word 'pigling' instead? Think of other names ending in 'ling'.

> A suffix added to a name in this way is called a **diminutive** because it denotes a smaller version. It isn't the only way; we don't say 'doglet' for example, but 'puppy'. Diminutives are also added to people's names to show familiarity and affection, but they can be annoying if you don't like the person doing it. The word 'love' for example, can be turned into 'lovey' (little love). Some mothers always refer to children as 'little loves' or 'lovies'. Many boys' and girls' names take diminutives: Joseph/Joe/Joey; Anthony/Tony; Anne/Annie; Margery/Marge/Margie. When people grow up, they sometimes hate being called by their diminutive name, even in the family. Do you have a diminutive name? Do you like it?

Think of a dozen or so nouns, including some names, that have diminutive forms. List them.

2   Many first names for girls are derived from the names of flowers and plants: Heather, Marigold, Jasmine. Find out some more names like these. Where do boys' names come from? Look up names of boys in your class.

What is the difference between Pear Blossom's name change and Abigail's in *Playing Beatie Bow*? (See Unit Ten).

3   Notice that Pear Blossom's name has been translated from Korean. Find names in the story that haven't been translated, but written as they would sound in Korean.

4   Look up the meanings of any of the following words you do not know: glossing, lustred, finery, unhulled (very unusual one, this), diligently, glistening, mountebanks, persimmons (another unusual one), bedraggled,

brocade, girdle, baldric (nothing whatever to do with Blackadder!), boudoir, fragrant.

5 What do you think these phrases mean? 'richly cultured'? 'high in office'?

6 Where in the story is the girl called Pear Blossom and where is she called Pigling? Why do you think the different names have been used in this way?

7 The stepsister is named at the very beginning as Violet, but how is she referred to in the rest of the story?

8 Does Mrs Kang Wa have a name? How is she referred to in the story?

9 What impressions do you get of Pear Blossom's father? Look at the first and the last paragraphs. Which words tell you about his appearance and behaviour?

10 What do you think the following phrase means: 'the gift from her stepmother of a rope of cash to spend for dainties'?
Would you say 'spend for'?

11 The translation of the original story is a little old-fashioned. Look at the following words: brute, gay.
Do you use them in the same way today? Would you call a cat 'a brute' or say that you went to a 'gay' party?

Do you think flowers might be important in Korean culture?

On what occasions in English life are flowers important?

Grammar and Punctuation

1 Find the following sentences and copy them out, numbering each one:
  a) Pear Blossom had been the name............left motherless. (Paragraph 1)
  b) When her father............was named Violet. (Paragraph 1)
  c) They were hateful............girl weep often. (Paragraph 1)
  d) So Pigling had time............snow-white. (Paragraph 9)
  e) Charming indeed............snow-white silk. (Paragraph 18)
  f) Nevertheless............of fragrant petals. (Paragraph 19)

When you have written out the sentences, find the following words in each sentence and put a circle round each one:
  a) who
  b) who
  c) which
  d) that
  e) which
  f) that

There are three different words here but they are all doing the same job. What do you think that job is? You can answer the question by looking back in the sentence to the word or phrase you think the 'who', the 'which' or the 'that' is referring to. Underline the word.

If you have got the right idea, you should have underlined the following words or phrases

    a) Pear Blossom
    b) her father Kang Wa
    c) called her Pigling
    d) plain but clean clothes
    e) long undersleeves
    f) a pear tree

> The words you have been investigating are called RELATIVE PRONOUNS or RELATIVES. This has nothing to do with your granny or your aunts and uncles but means that the word relates two parts of a sentence.

The main relative pronouns are: who, whom, whose, which, that.
They enable you to make your writing less boring and more grown up. Here is an example of the difference relative pronouns make:

You could write:

My friend is a great runner. He has won lots of trophies. His mum keeps them in a cabinet in the hall.

Or you could write:

My friend is a great runner who has won lots of trophies which his mum keeps in a cabinet in the hall.

What's the difference?

Look at the following sets of short sentences and connect them using relative pronouns:

  a) This is the house. Jack built the house.
  b) He was an amazing driver. He won every Grand Prix held in 1956.
  c) This is the old woman. She owns the dog. The dog ate the cat. The cat ate the mouse. The mouse ate the spider. The spider ate the fly. The fly wriggled and jiggled and tickled inside her. The old woman swallowed the fly.
  d) She is the ringleader. She caused all the trouble. I was blamed for it.
  e) The head wanted to see the pupils. Their bikes had been vandalised.

Don't mix up 'whose' with 'who's'. 'Whose' is a relative pronoun; 'Who's' is a question; – 'who is . . .?' or 'Who has . . .?'. Check with your teacher if you don't understand this.

'Whom' is an odd one that may well be going out of fashion in writing. It already sounds old-fashioned in speech. At one time it was considered correct to say: 'To whom were you speaking in the corridor?' 'I do not know to whom I spoke'.
Nowadays, a teacher is more likely to say (quite correctly): 'Who were you speaking to in the corridor?' And you would most likely reply (quite correctly): 'I do not know who I was speaking to'. But the ghost of a pupil from a hundred years ago might well have replied: 'I do not know to whom I was speaking, Sir'.

The word 'whom' has not entirely gone out of the English language. It can be found in the title of a novel by Ernest Hemingway, *For Whom The Bell Tolls* and on envelopes and at the top of messages; To Whom It May Concern. Notice that it is almost always preceded by a word such as: from, with, by, to, for, under, over. In other words – by a preposition.

Before we leave the subject of relative pronouns, look at the following sentences:

> **a)** Wally gave it to his brother who lives in Canada.
> **b)** Wally gave it to his brother, who lives in Canada.

You can see a relative pronoun here, relating back to 'brother', but what difference does the comma make?
Here is a clue: How many brothers has Wally got in (a) and how many has he got in (b)?

Check with your teacher if you can't work out what the comma does.

2   Look at the following sentence:

With her tears dried, Pigling followed this wonderful brute out over the meadows into the woods, where she found the most delicious fruit her eyes ever rested upon.

Notice the 'where' that neatly connects 'the woods' to the 'delicious fruit' she found in them. This is another of those 'wh' words that are so useful but it isn't a relative pronoun, it is an adverb of place. (Remember, adverbs always tell you when, where or how).

The sentence could have been written as follows:

With her tears dried, Pigling followed this wonderful brute out over the meadows into the woods. In the woods she found the most delicious fruit her eyes ever rested upon.

Look at the pairs of sentences below and connect them into one sentence, using the adverb 'where':

a) I went into Glebe Street. The Taylor family lived there.

b) I want to see the Grand Theatre. My grandfather used to sing in the Grand Theatre.

c) Isn't that the castle? Didn't they imprison traitors there?

3   Look at paragraph five which consists of two sentences. Look at the first word of each sentence. One is a question word and the sentence is a question, the other *looks* like a question word but the sentence isn't a question. Which is which?
Write two sentences beginning with the word 'what', that aren't questions. Two old advertising slogans will give you an idea: an advertisement for beer (*What we want is Watneys!*) and an advertisement for Smarties, and note the unusual spellings (*Wotalotigot!*).

Exclamations often begin with word 'What . . .'
e.g. 'What a goal!'
     "What a swizz!'
     'What a shame!'

4   Of the first 14 paragraphs of this tale, five begin with adverbs. Which are they, and what do the adverbs do? Four of them are single words, one is a phrase.

5   There is a question in paragraph five. Who asks it?

6   Is there any dialogue in this tale? Would you have liked more?

Your own writing

Choose one of the following writing tasks:

1   Write a modern version of the story, setting it in your own town or neighbourhood. Keep the plot but change the characters. It could be a stepbrother, for example, and it doesn't have to be a cow that provides all the lovely food. It doesn't even have to be food.
Make sure your tale begins and ends well, and that there is a point to it. Remember that your reader should enjoy it.

2   At the end of the story, Violet and her mother have disappeared from the scene. Rewrite the story from Violet's point of view. You can keep her as a 'baddy' or make her a 'goodie'.

UNIT FIFTEEN: *Speaking and Writing*

TEXTS: TRANSCRIPTS AND EXCERPTS FROM WRITTEN TEXTS

Readings: An anthology of thirteen examples

First:
- Text One: Transcript of someone instructing in the use of a computer
- Text Two: Page from a computer game manual

Then excerpts from:

- Text Three: *Dick Tracy* cartoon strip
- Text Four: Transcript of a group of boys talking
- Text Five: Speech by Martin Luther King
- Text Six: *Finest Hour* – two excerpts
- Text Seven: *Romeo and Juliet*
- Text Eight: Transcript of a girl telling about an incident
- Text Nine: From Tony Blair's Labour Conference speech
- Text Ten: *Only Fools and Horses*
- Text Eleven: Transcript of a telephone conversation
- Text Twelve: Advertisements
- Text Thirteen: *Olive Senior* story

1   This unit gives you an opportunity to compare everyday speech as it happens (i.e. as you open your mouth and just do it) with speech that was written down in the first place, as in a play for example.

Until the invention of tape recorders, speech was something that was lost forever the moment it had been spoken. There were audio typists who could type, at amazing speed, what people said, as they said it, and there was also shorthand. But the tape recorder has made it possible to capture the sound of every word spoken. That means, not just what someone *thought* had been said, but what had *actually* been said and *how* it was said.

Think what a difference it would make to our understanding of Shakespeare's day, if tape recorders (and film cameras) had been invented then.

> Once you have a tape recording of what someone has said, you can **transcribe** their words; write down very exactly what they said. This kind of writing is called a **transcript**.

Transcripts are not normally punctuated, except for proper nouns, because punctuation marks belong to writing, not speech. A few have been used here to help you understand what is meant, e.g. questions.

The brackets tell you that the speaker has paused, and when something has been said loudly, it can be written in capital letters. Where two people speak at once, a bracket sign is usually used.

Some parts of a transcript can be difficult for a reader to follow, though anyone listening at the time would have had no difficulty.

Playscripts and **dialogue in stories** are much easier to read because they were written to be read in the first place. Even actors have to be able to read the script they are acting out. Scripts are written for speakers to read aloud. Dialogue in stories is written for readers.

Do remember that writing is not better than speech. It's not worse either, just different. You can do some things in speech that you can't do in writing, and you can do some things in writing that you can't do in speech. Obviously they use the same English vocabulary and grammar, but in different ways and in different circumstances.

Now look at the two texts (Texts One and Two) below. The first is a transcript of someone explaining to a friend how to save work on to a floppy disk. The second comes from the Training Manual of a Star Trek computer game. Work with a partner and list all the ways you can think of in which speech and writing are different. Pay attention to ways in which spoken sentences are different from written ones. Try to describe the differences you have noticed.

Don't go on to the other texts until you have studied these two texts.

Set out your thoughts and ideas using a table like the one below:

SPEECH	WRITING

TEXT ONE

Well erm you've got to put your disk in first ( ) that programs it ( ) right? see there's your files come up on the screen ( ) right ( ) now take it out and put in your floppy ( ) that's right ( ) no ( ) hang on ( ) you've got it in the wrong way round ( ) we'll mark this side so you'll know ( ) right ( ) put it back in ( ) now you can save on this disk right? ( ) but don't forget to press F1 to tell it you've changed the disk ( ) there ( ) the screen's changed looks a bit full to me this ( ) do you need all these files?

From an A level student's coursework on Computerspeak

TEXT TWO

The Forward Bridge View

Most of your time on the Bridge will be spent in the command chair. From this vantage point, you will see the main view screen centred above the Navigation and Weapons Control console.

View screen: Use this in conjunction with the Radar Screen to keep track of the tactical picture.

> **Learning to target enemy ships quickly with the kypd "0" (Ins) and kypad "." (Del) keys is absolutely crucial to your ships survival.**

If you move your mouse cursor over the view screen, it will change to the view screen symbol. When it does, left click and you will shift to the full screen view. You can also press F3 to go to full screen. Some Captains prefer to fight the ship from this view and a small mockup of the radar screen and weapons ready monitor (see explanation below) is provided in the upper right hand corner to facilitate those options. The currently targeted object appears as a wire frame model on the display above a wire frame of your own ship. Each displays approximations of the damage it has received.

To exit this view and return to the normal bridge screen, move your mouse cursor to the bottom of the screen and left click or press F3.

W A R N I N G

If you enter a gravity well you will lose your ship. Planets appear on radar as grey/white large circles. Do not run into them.

Finally, from the forward bridge view, if you move your mouse cursor to the top of the screen, it will change into the captain's log symbol. Left click and you can pull up a complete listing of the messages and reports you have received during the current mission. To close this box, simply press ESC or click previous.

When you have finished your table, do the following:

a) Name two advantages that spoken instructions have over written ones.

b) Name two advantages that written instructions have over spoken ones.

c) What differences did you find between spoken and written sentences? Why do you think there are these differences?

2 Now look at another series of short texts (Texts 3 to 13). Some are transcripts, some are dialogue written for readers.

When you have read them, re-organise them to show which ones you think are closest to natural, everyday speech, and which ones are closest to writing. You can do this in a table using three columns. In the first column (a narrow one) put the number of the text; in the second put whether it is a transcript, a playscript (i.e. written for speaking) or story dialogue; in the third column put one or two good reasons for deciding whether it is a transcript, a script or story dialogue.

Remember, you are re-ordering them from closest to natural speech down to furthest from natural speech. One has been done for you.

Your table should look like this:

Text	Type of Speech	Language Clues to the Type of Speech
4	Transcript	no punctuation / two people speak at once / haven't a clue what 'it' or 'that stuff' is

Compare your list and comments with other people's. If there are some differences, that's fine. Discuss them. There is no reason at all why you shouldn't notice different things. Your teacher will have a suggested list, with which you can compare yours.

TEXT THREE

The following is part of a comic strip story featuring the American supercop, Dick Tracy.

TEXT FOUR

Two boys are helping out in a room badly in need of repairs and decoration. They are waiting for their friend who has gone to get something they need.

Kevin: hi I've got one took ages
Dave: hi ( ) mind all the stuff
Kevin: you've got a lot done
Dave: Colin's given us a hand
Colin: hi
Kevin: hi
Dave: where'd you get it?
Kevin: Holroyd's
Dave: give us it 'ere
Colin: is this coming out?
Dave: what? er no ( ) leave that ( ) thanks Kev
Kevin: is it right?
Dave: yeah
Colin: what needs doing next?
Dave: let's knock off for a brew
Colin: great idea
Kevin: look I'm a bit pushed ( ) I'll come back this aft ( ) Gavin 'n' Simon'll help
Colin: it's nearly off this
Dave: it'll plaster back in again ( ) don't make it worse

TEXT FIVE

The following text on page 119 is part of a speech delivered by Martin Luther King in 1963 at a civil rights march on Washington, USA.

I say to you today, my friends, that in spite of the difficulties and frustrations of the moment I still have a dream. It is a dream deeply rooted in the American dream.

I have a dream that one day this nation will rise up and live out the true meaning of its creed: 'We hold these truths to be self-evident; that all men are created equal.'

I have a dream that one day on the red hills of Georgia the sons of former slaves and the sons of former slaveowners will be able to sit down together at the table of brotherhood . . .

I have a dream that my four little children will one day live in a nation where they will not be judged by the color of their skin but by the content of their character . . .

I have a dream today . . .

TEXT SIX

The following are two eyewitness accounts of German attacks on British convoys in the Atlantic, 1940. Both accounts were related to an interviewer: the first is a sailor's vivid recollection of seeing a ship blown up; the second tells of a young girl's experience after the ship taking her to safety (!) in America was sunk. Clinging onto a capsized lifeboat, she is finally picked up by another lifeboat.

(a)

Then I saw the Basilisk sinking over on our starboard side, then the Skipjack went, she was a sloop. Ships were sinking all around us, everywhere you could see destroyers going down with this terrific attack. And as she started to really lurch I couldn't get the gun elevated properly, but we hung on because when the bombers had gone these fighter planes came down and they started strafing anyone in the water or on the decks. And while I am watching I saw the St Abbs with all the survivors including our Captain. She hadn't got very far and they got a bomb right down her funnel. The whole bloody lot went sky high. They were all in the water again, well those that got blown over the side. And already in the water you'd got survivors from five or six ships. Some were soldiers. And great big pools of black oil. They were all floundering around in the oil screaming and yelling.

(b)

Closer and closer it came and then men inside it were cheering and shouting and saying, 'Hang on, hang on, we're coming'. We could hear noises coming from the destroyer too and it sounded like a rugby crowd. Men were cheering and shouting. These sailors had been picking dead children up all day and to find us alive was like a miracle. The coxswain of the lifeboat, to whom I shall ever be grateful, a chap called Albert Gorman, stretched his hands out and said to me, 'Come on darling, let go.' Do you know I couldn't let go. My hands were stuck tight.

From *Finest Hour* by Tim Clayton and Phil Craig (Hodder & Stoughton, 2000)

TEXT SEVEN

The following is an extract from Act Two, Scene Two of Shakespeare's *Romeo and Juliet.*

Juliet:	How camest thou hither, tell me, and wherefore?
	The orchard walls are high, and hard to climb,
	And the place death, considering who thou art,
	If any of my kinsmen find thee here.
Romeo:	With love's light wings did I o'erperch these walls;
	For stony limits cannot hold love out,
	And what love can do that dares love attempt;
	Therefore, thy kinsmen are no let to me.
Juliet:	If they do see thee, they will murder thee.
Romeo:	Alack, there lies more peril in thine eye
	Than twenty of their swords: look thou but sweet,
	And I am proof against their enmity.
Juliet:	I would not for the world they saw thee here.
Romeo:	I have night's cloak to hide me from their sight;
	And thou but love me, let them find me here:
	My life were better ended by their hate,
	Than death prorogued, wanting of thy love.

TEXT EIGHT

A girl is telling her friends about a minor mishap while on holiday on the Norfolk Broads.

so I er ( ) well you know ( ) I sort of swung it round too hard and ( ) oh no before that I hadn't pulled back the throttle ( ) well I thought I had ( ) so I was going too fast ( ) look there's one just like ours only without this awning thing ( ) I think that is the trouble you know you can't see out properly ( ) anyway it bumped and he went mad and he said get off the boat ( ) there wasn't any damage ( ) I got it in neutral ( ) right ( ) and it cut out ( ) I said I was sorry and I picked up all the things ( ) but he's just not ( ) er well I'm not his favourite person at the moment.

From a student's coursework folder.

TEXT NINE

The following are two excerpts from Prime Minister Blair's speech to the Labour Party Conference in Brighton, 2000.

(a)

The second big choice: a Government with the strength to help people through change, or a Government that leaves you to fend for yourself.

And because of the scale of what we are doing, and the scale of our ambition, let me set out in detail what we are doing, and what we will do in the future.

Because 90 per cent of new jobs will need skills with computers, there will be 6,000 centres round Britain, giving access to the internet and help with technology. Everyone will get an 80 per cent discount on computer courses, the unemployed will get it for free. There will be 1,000 more technology centres for small businesses or the self-employed.

Because we want to stay ahead in the new technologies we are investing £2 billion over five years in British science, the largest investment since the 1960s.

Because we know small businesses are a big part of the future, we are setting up venture capital funds in every region, tax breaks for investment, cuts in small business tax and the new Small Business Service to act as their advocate and protector in Government.

And because we know the danger that in a changing world new forms of inequality and social exclusion are created: the Sure Start programme – £500 million – to help children in poverty; a new Careers Service for school leavers; cutting homelessness and helping the homeless get jobs; a £1 billion programme to renew deprived neighbourhoods; and extending the New Deal in the unemployment blackspots of Britain.

(b)

The third big choice: a Government with the strength to invest for the long term, or a Government that cuts our public services.

The next stage on the journey requires not only excellent primary schools but first-class secondary schools.

By 2004, there will be 1,000 specialist schools. An extra billion pound investment in ICT, to ensure one computer to every five children in our secondary schools.

Catch-up tuition for all 11 and 12 year olds who arrive without good literacy and numeracy. New targets for 14 and 16 year olds.

Better incentives for staying on at school, and an overhaul of further education to raise standards.

Today I make a further commitment. Line one in the next manifesto will be a promise to increase the share of our national wealth spent on education in the next Parliament.

Education. Education. Education. Then. Now. And in the future.

TEXT TEN

Rodney and Del Trotter and Uncle Albert are at home. Del has given Rodney a battered, old typewriter so that he can write a script for a film.

Del: Away you go then

Rodney: Away I go what?

Del: Well, you know, you know, start the old typing.

Albert: Yeah, be creative.

Rodney: Be creat . . . I can't just be creative at the drop of a hat can I? There are certain things a writer needs before he can actually start writing. Like a story!

Albert: You ain't even got a story?!

Rodney: Not exactly, I've only been trying for a few days ain't I?

Del: Listen, I've had an idea for a story and it's a bloody good'un an' all! D'you wanna hear it?

Rodney: No . . . not really Del.

Albert: Oh that's charming innit? You buy him a brand-new typewriter and come up with a story for him, and what thanks do you get?

Rodney: Alright, tell us yer story then.

Del: No, no, don't bother yourself Rodney, please. I was only trying to help you.

Rodney: Oh now, come on, honestly Del, seriously, I'd like to hear your story . . . Well, I need a bit of help, don't I?

Del: Right, okay, now this is a 'Jaws' type story.

Rodney: 'Jaws'??? 'Jaws' has been done though.

Del: I know it's been done! But this is different. It's called . . . 'There's a Rhino Loose in the City'.

Rodney: (stares at Del incredulously) There's a Rhi . . . There's a Rhino Loose In . . . A Rhino? As in rhinoceros?

Del: That's right. 'There's A Rhino Loose In The City'.

Albert: What's it about Del?

Del: Well, it's about this rhinoceros right, escapes from a zoo and it heads straight for London! And after two or three days they find all these dead bodies lying about and no-one knows who who's done it! So, they get hold of this private detective, you know, like a sort of Charlton Heston type geezer to try and solve the crime. Now the zoo keeper happens to be a very attractive woman. Before you know where you are, old Charlton is giving the sort what for, so there's your romantic interest!

Rodney: A rhinoceros??

Del: Yeah! But they don't know it's missing!

Rodney: But how can you not know Del?? If you've got a rhinoceros right and one day it ain't there – well, you tend to know it's missing!!

Del: Don't be a plonker all yer life Rodney. She ain't got one rhinoceros, she probably had two or three rhinoceroses.

Albert: And how's he escape?

Rodney: Squeezed through the bars most probably!

Del: Don't you start getting saucy with me Rodney, I'm only trying to help you.

---

continued

> *Rodney:* I don't believe this! Nobody knows it's escaped? What about the eight million people living in London? Don't none of them spot it?
> *Del:* Yes! But the ones who spot it – they're the ones who get trampled to death!
> *Rodney:* And what about all the others? The people sitting in offices, the people in cafes, the people sitting on top of buses! It's a rhino Del.
> *Del:* He only comes out at night.
> *Albert:* What is it, a vampire rhino?
> *Del:* No it is not a vampire rhino. That's stupid that is, innit eh?

From *Video Nasty*, an episode of 'Only Fools and Horses' by John Sullivan (BBC Books, 1999)

TEXT ELEVEN

A caller is having a problem dialling the right number, and has rung Directory Enquiries:

> *Caller:* ah the thing is this is a bit of a mystery. I've been trying this number for two days ( ) um yesterday somebody told me to put 58 in front of it ( ) which got me a very unusual dialling ( ) situation ( ) I haven't been able to get through and I'm you know I have a letter from a large company saying he's there waiting for me to phone and I CAN'T GET THROUGH
>
> *Operator:* yes ( ) well 58 should be put in front of some numbers but these um ( ) let me just read this ( ) you've tried it with 58 in front?
>
> *Caller:* yes
>
> *Operator:* oh I should dial 100 and ask the operator to help you then because um ( ) you know if you dial it with 58 in front it should certainly be all right
>
> *Caller:* but I should be able to dial it without the 58 in front?
>
> *Operator:* just a moment let me read this list here properly no you should have the 58 in front of it
>
> *Caller:* I should have the 58 in front
>
> *Operator:* yes yes and I'll check the code for you while you're on the line perhaps it's the code you see ( ) your code should be 0908
>
> *Caller:* yes that's what I've been dialling
>
> *Operator:* and then 58 and then the number ( ) that should definitely be all right
>
> *Caller:* yes I I've got a feeling there's something going on on the exchange there because it gives a very funny very sort of you know it dials then stops

From *The Psychology of Language and Communication* by Andrew Ellis and Geoffrey Beattie (Psychology Press, 1986)

TEXT TWELVE

Below are some advertising texts:

No time to join a readers' group, but would like to share a book you have read with others? Would you like to try a book someone else has read in return? Why not try a **Book Chain**?

What is a Book Chain?
A great way of discovering different kinds of books and authors you may not have read before. Better still, each book comes with a brief comment from another reader.

How does it work?
You pick a book, read it, write a few lines about it and pass it on. You then receive somebody else's choice with their comments. The library staff arrange the exchanges so the book chain members remain anonymous to each other.

How long does a chain last?
Approximately three months but it will vary. There are no time limits. You will probably read 2 or 3 books other than your own choice in that time.

What if I hate one of the books?
Don't read it. But do write your comments on the sheet anyway, so that the next reader knows what you thought.

Do I get a chance to see what other people in other chains are reading and what they think about their books?
Yes! At the end of the chain, comments will be displayed on our readers' notice board.

Can I meet the other members of the chain?
If you'd like to. Please let library staff know.

How do I join the Book Chain?
Just fill in the tear-off portion of this leaflet and hand it in to a member of staff.

IF You Have Indigestion

Alkalize stomach instantly this amazing NEW way

DR. SMITH TOLD US TO USE "MILK OF MAGNESIA". IT ALKALIZES AN ACID CONDITION ALMOST IMMEDIATELY

ACID INDIGESTION HAS SPOILED MANY A GOOD TIME FOR ME. I'M GLAD TO KNOW HOW YOU OBTAINED RELIEF

On every side to-day people are being urged to *alkalize* the stomach to ease the symptoms of "acid indigestion," nausea and stomach upsets. For the vast majority of stomach upsets come from an excess of acidity.

To gain quick alkalization, just do this: Take two teaspoonfuls of 'Milk of Magnesia' after eating. OR—take two 'Milk of Magnesia' brand Tablets, which have the same antacid effect.

Relief comes almost at once. Nausea; flatulence—fulness after eating and "acid indigestion" quickly disappear. You feel like a new person. Try this way. You'll be surprised at the results. Get either the liquid preparation or the remarkable new 'Milk of Magnesia' brand Tablets. They're delightful to take and easy to carry with you.

Sold by all Chemists.
'Milk of Magnesia' 1/3 and 2/6 (*Treble Size*)
Also 'Milk of Magnesia' brand Tablets 6d., 1/-, 2/- and 3/6.

'MILK OF MAGNESIA'

(Regd.)

'Milk of Magnesia' is the trade mark of Phillips' preparation of Magnesia.

can't think what to give her this Christmas

why not a Hoover? she's always wanted one

fougasse

— THIS *Christmas* you can have a Hoover for £10·15

OR ONLY 10/- DOWN

Every woman would like to have The Hoover—because she knows it's the best. This Christmas for the first time every woman can! And no husband can invest 10/- to better purpose. Alternatively, for £1 down you can have the Jubilee Hoover—the finest cleaner in the world. Send the coupon for booklet now.

✱ DUSTING TOOLS £2. 2. 6 EXTRA

From a Kirklees Metropolitan Council publication, 2000

TEXT THIRTEEN

Beccka is a very independent-minded young girl. Earlier in the story, the author says 'she just stick out her tongue at the world and wink at God'. The Archdeacon is visiting her home. The family are all in their best clothes and Beccka is trying to be on her best behaviour.

By now Beccka and the Archdeacon exchanging Bible knowledge. Beccka asking him question and he trying his best to answer but they never really tell him any of these things in theological college. First he go ask Beccka if she is a good little girl. Beccka say yes she read her Bible every day. Do you now say the Archdeacon, splendid. Beccka smile and look shy.

'Tell me my little girl, is there anything in the bible you would like to ask me about?'

'Yes sir. Who in the Bible wrote big?'

'Who in the Bible wrote big. My dear child!'

This wasnt the kind of question Archdeacon expecting but him always telling himself how he have rapport with children so he decide to confess his ignorance.

'Tell me, who?'

'Paul!' Beccka shout.

'Paul?'

'Galatians six eleven "See with how large letters I write onto you with mine own hands".'

'Ho Ho Ho Ho' Archdeacon laugh. – 'Well done. Try me with another one.'

Beccka decide to ease him up this time.

'What animal saw an angel?'

'What animal saw an angel? My word. What animal . . . of course. Balaam's ass.'

'Yes you got it.'

Beccka jumping up and down she so excited. She decide to ask the Archdeacon a trick questions her father did teach her.

'What did Adam and Eve do when they were driven out of the garden?'

'Hm,' the Archdeacon sputtered but could not think of a suitable answer.

'Raise Cain ha ha ha ha ha.'

'They raised Cain Ho Ho Ho Ho Ho.'

The Archdeacon promise himself to remember that one to tell the Deacon. All the same he not feeling strictly comfortable. It really dont seem dignified for an Archdeacon to be having this type of conversation with an eleven-year-old girl. But Beccka already in high gear with the next question and Archdeacon tense himself.

'Who is the shortest man in the Bible?'

Archdeacon groan.

'Peter. Because him sleep on his watch. Ha Ha Ha.'

'Ho Ho Ho Ho Ho.'

'What is the smallest insect in the Bible?'

'The widow's mite,' Archdeacon shout.

continued

'The wicked flee,' Beccka cry.

'Ho Ho Ho Ho Ho Ho.'

Archdeacon laughing so hard now he starting to cough. He cough and cough till the coughing bring him to his senses. He there looking down the passage where Auntie Mary gone and wish she would hurry come back. He sputter a few time into his handkerchief, wipe his eye, sit up straight and assume his most religious expression. Even Beccka impress.

'Now Rebecca. Hm. You are a very clever very entertaining little girl. Very. But what I had in mind were questions that are a bit more serious. Your aunt tells me you are being prepared for confirmation. Surely you must have some questions about doctrine hm, religion, that puzzle you. No serious questions?'

Beccka look at Archdeacon long and hard. 'Yes,' she say at long last in a small voice. Right away Archdeacon sit up straighter.

'What is it my little one?'

Beccka screwing up her face in concentration.

'Sir, what I want to know is this for I cant find it in the Bible. Please sir, do angels wear brassieres?'

Auntie Mary just that minute coming through the doorway with a full tea tray with Cherry carrying another big tray right behind her. Enough food and drink for ten Archdeacon. Auntie Mary stops braps in the doorway with fright when she hear Beccka question. She stop so sudden that Cherry bounce into her and spill a whole pitcher of cold drink all down Auntie Mary back. As the coldness hit her Auntie Mary jump and half her tray throw way on the floor milk and sugar and sandwiches a rain down on Archdeacon. Archdeacon jump up with his handkerchief and start mop himself and Auntie Mary at the same time he trying to take the tray from her. Auntie Mary at the same time trying to mop up the Archdeacon with a napkin in her mortification not even noticing how Archdeacon relieve that so much confusion come at this time. Poor soft-hearted Cherry only see that her sister whole life ruin now she dont yet know the cause run and sit on the kitchen stool and throw kitchen cloth over her head and sit there bawling and bawling in sympathy.

From *Do Angels Wear Brassieres?* in 'Summer Lightning' by Olive Senior

When you have storted out all the texts into transcripts, playscripts and story dialogues, answer the following questions about the texts, and do the activities.

TEXT ONE: Questions

1   Why do you think so many spoken explanations and instructions begin with 'well'? Why is it such a popular word? Do you use it?

2   Choose a day this week, or next, and keep a special ear open for where, when and how people use the word 'well'. Collect examples from teacher talk, pupil talk, parents' talk, family talk, friends' talk.

3 Which is the most frequently used pronoun? Why? Is any other pronoun used? Why?

4 What kinds of sentences are there? Imperatives? Questions? Statements?

TEXT TWO: Questions

1 Go through this text and list the things that make a written text (including pictures) especially useful.

2 Make a note of any words and phrases, or layout features, that need to be used in written texts but which could hardly be used in spoken instructions.

3 Look again at the spoken instructions in Text One. Write them out for a manual in the style of the Star Trek instructions.

TEXT THREE: Questions

1 Apart from the names of the artists, there are two words in this comic strip which are not in speech or thought bubbles. Which are they, and why are they there?

2 How do you know which words are thoughts and which ones are spoken?

3 Why are some words in bold letters?

4 What is a 'black and white'?

5 Write out the storyline from picture 1 to picture 12. Tell it in a mixture of your own words and words from the comic strip. Imagine you are writing the beginning of a detective story. You could begin like this:

> Groovy Jones walked up the stairs to Lizz's apartment. He was five minutes early but he hoped she wouldn't mind. The door was ajar.
> 'That's funny,' he thought.
> When he went in . . .

TEXT FOUR: Questions

1 Find the following words in the text: one, stuff, it, this, that, It's, this, It'll, it. It is perfectly clear that the boys know what they mean, why don't you? Why wouldn't any reader?

2 Look at the places where two people speak together. Does this ever happen to you? Are there times when it doesn't matter, and times where it does?

3 Write out the transcript as though it were a scene in a TV comedy. Use normal punctuation and write some simple instructions for the camera operators and the set designer so that the use of words like 'this' and 'that' will be clear to the audience. Here is an example to help you. Two characters, David and Colin, are getting a room ready for decorating. There is a pile of old plaster and wallpaper near the door. Kevin enters holding up a trowel for re-plastering. He is very pleased with himself.

KEVIN:	*Hi. I've got one. It took ages.* (He doesn't notice the rubbish)
DAVE:	*Hi. Mind all that stuff.*
KEVIN:	*You've got a lot done.*
DAVE:	*Colin's given us a hand.*
COLIN:	(standing on an old chair and struggling with a wooden panel) *Hi.*

TEXT FIVE: Questions

1   This is a famous, historic speech and now a famous and historic piece of writing. What clues are there to tell you that it was originally written to be delivered as a speech? Read it aloud to hear what it might have sounded like – even though you may not have a Black American accent!

2   How important are the repetitions? What effect do they have?

3   Compare this political speech with the political speech of Text Nine. Do they have anything in common? What are they both trying to do?

TEXT SIX (a) and (b): Questions

1   Both of these texts tell of terrible events that happen when an Atlantic convoy is attacked by German submarines. The interviewer has tidied up what the speakers said in order to make it easier to read. How do you know that both were originally spoken and not written? How can you tell it was spoken to an interviewer?

2   The first speaker is remembering what he saw of a terrible event. Which words show his emotion?

3   The second speaker is imagining something that happened to her as a child. How do you know that she is now an adult?

4   What two different tenses are used in the fourth sentence of the first speech? Is this a 'mistake'? Why might it have happened?

5   How many sentences in the first speech begin with the word 'And'? Why?

6   At the beginning of the second speech, there are a number of present participle verbs. They give a vivid picture of what was going on. Find them and list them, including any repetitions.

7   Why do you think 'Do you know' is used a lot in conversation? Can you imagine the way in which it might have been said in the second speech? How would you say it, if you were beginning something with, 'Do you know . . .'?

8   If it is new to you, check out the meaning of the word 'coxswain'. How is it pronounced? Compare it with another naval word, 'boatswain'.

TEXT SEVEN: Questions

1 What kind of talk is this? Where would you find it? When was it written?

2 The English here is over 400 years old. List some of the things that sound 'old-fashioned' to you. One word, for example, you may find difficult is 'prorogued'. It means 'terminated'! What other word can you find in 'prorogued'? (notice its unusual spelling). Another word, 'pilot', couldn't possibly have meant to Shakespeare what it means to most people nowadays.

3 Rewrite the scene in modern English. Make sure you first understand what the Elizabethan English means.

TEXT EIGHT: Questions

1 Everyday, perfectly intelligent speech, like this example, contains lots of things you don't find in writing. How many can you find in this example? List them.

2 At the end there is a remark that begins with the pronoun 'he' and then changes to the pronoun 'I'. It would be a mistake in writing, but it often happens in speech. Why do you think it has happened here?

3 Imagine that the speaker, later on, told the story in a letter to another friend. It wouldn't be the same. Write the letter she might have written.

TEXT NINE: Questions

1 Read aloud, slowly and carefully, the two excerpts from Tony Blair's Labour Conference speech in order to make sure you understand just what it says. Check any words or ideas and phrases you don't understand. What are the points that come across most strongly?

2 List words and phrases in the excerpts that refer to the future.

3 Are there any repetitions in the excerpts?

4 How do you think the colon in the first paragraph of the second excerpt would have come across in actual speech?

5 The middle part of the second excerpt is mainly a list of things. What happens in the next to last paragraph (the penultimate one)?

6 What happens in the last paragraph? Where are the verbs?

7 Look at the repeated grammatical structure in the first excerpt. Write three paragraphs that begin in the same way. Imagine you are giving reasons for longer school holidays or something similar.

TEXT TEN: Questions

1 What does the scriptwriter, John Sullivan, do to make the dialogue sound like real speech? List the sorts of things people often say in real life.

2 Read the text aloud with a partner. You should enjoy it. Imagine you were doing it for radio.

3 What does Rodney really think about Del's story? How do you know?

TEXT ELEVEN: Questions

1 You will find it easier to follow the transcript if you act it out with a partner, one taking the part of the caller, the other taking the part of the operator. When you have done this, discuss with your partner whether or not the speakers are communicating clearly. Can you understand the caller's problem? Is the operator being helpful?

2 Look for the following four phrases: 'the thing is'; 'just a moment'; 'sort of'; 'you know'. They crop up a lot in conversations, especially the last one. You are hardly ever likely to see them in formal writing, except as dialogue in a play or a story. Why are they used so often? What do they do? Remember, there is usually a good reason.

3 Telephone conversations have been described as a half-way house between ordinary speech and writing. Think of some of the ways this could be true. What is there in telephone conversations that is like ordinary conversations, and what is there that is closer to writing?

TEXT TWELVE: Questions

1 For a long time printed advertisements have been made to sound like people are talking. TV advertisements of course, can have it both ways: speaking and writing. Two of the advertisements here are old-fashioned ones from the 1930s, both selling something. The third is a modern advertisement by Kirklees Libraries informing readers about a good idea that is absolutely free. All three use speech to persuade the reader. What are the differences in the ways that they do it?

2 In the two old-fashioned advertisements there are two pairs of people talking and also a third voice that is speaking to you, whose is this voice? Working in threes, read the advertisements aloud as though you were advertising on commercial radio. Two of you speak the words of the 'characters' and one of you speak the advertiser's voice. Make it lively so that somebody tuning in would actually listen.

3 Collect advertisements in modern newspapers, magazines and leaflets that use this technique. Why do you think it continues to be popular?

4 Now look at the library leaflet advertising a Book Chain. What is the technique that it uses seven times?
It is another popular technique for informing people about something: a question and answer dialogue.
What do you think is the advantage of this technique? Read it aloud to a

partner with the questions left in; and then read it aloud with all the questions left out. Discuss with your partner what difference the questions make.

5 Collect advertisements and information leaflets that use the Question/Answer technique and compare how they do it.

TEXT THIRTEEN: Questions

1 Among the world's Englishes is a group known as Caribbean English which includes Jamaican English, Bahamian English, Barbadian/Bajan English, Trinidadian English. The writer of this story is Jamaican. You may speak Jamaican English yourself, or you may speak a British English, for example Scots, Welsh or Irish English.

Whatever your language background, look through this excerpt and list ways in which the grammar of Jamaican English differs from the grammar of standard British English.

2 What tense is the story written in? What effect does this have?

3 Much of this text is conversation. Point out some of the ways in which the writer herself tells the reader something. Pick one or two bits you like. Here is an example: 'Archdeacon laughing so hard now he starting to cough'.

4 There are some references to the Bible in this text. You will find them as follows:

a) 'You see how large a letter I have written unto you with mine own hand', St Paul's Epistle to the Galatians.
b) 'And the ass saw the angel of the Lord', The Book of Numbers, Chapter 22, verses 22 and 23.
c) 'Peter was keeping night watch', St Mark's Gospel, Chapter 14.
d) 'And there came a certain poor widow, and she threw three mites' (tiny coins), St Mark's Gospel, Chapter 12, verse 42.
e) 'The wicked flee when no man pursueth; but the righteous are bold as a lion', Proverbs, Chapter 28.

The term 'raising Cain' nowadays means 'reacting very angrily and drastically'. After God expelled Adam and Eve from the Garden, they had two sons, Cain and Abel. Later, Cain murdered Abel.

5 Do you know any awful puns or word jokes like Beccka's? Think of two or three; they do not have to be Biblical.
Now write a scene from a story in which a young boy or girl is telling her awful jokes to a visiting relative. Write the dialogue and some description of how the child tells the jokes and how the relative reacts.

UNIT SIXTEEN: *A Last Word on Sentences*

In this last unit you will look at some key terms in English grammar, and find out what they mean. They are: SUBJECT (sometimes called AGENT), CLAUSE and OBJECT.

If you have been working through these units you will have learned something about three aspects of language:

- **Words**, their meanings and spellings
- **Sentences**, what they do and how they are constructed
- **Texts**, words and sentences woven into continuous stories, poems and plays, information, arguments and instructions.

> GRAMMAR is the magic ingredient that links words, sentences and texts, gives them jobs to do and keeps everything tidy. It provides shapes to put your words and ideas in (sentences), and it provides shapes to put all your sentences in (texts).

The grammar jobs (word classes) that you have met in the units are

- NOUNS (the 'thingies', including noun phrases)
- VERBS (the action)
- ADVERBS that tell you more about the verbs (When? Where? How?)
- ADJECTIVES that describe the 'thingies'
- PRONOUNS (who's who and what's what)
- PREPOSITIONS and CONJUNCTIONS that fasten everything together.

> If you read a text wearing your grammar glasses, you can get an X-ray vision of the grammar skeleton. Two things are absolutely essential for the construction of a sentence and they are called the **subject** (or **agent**) and the **main verbs**. This is the sentence skeleton and your 'Grammar Ray' glasses will help you see it.

Subjects (or agents) are usually pronouns, nouns or noun phrases, which makes good sense because they are the people or the things that do the verb. You may prefer the word 'agent' to subject, so use it if you do. They are the same thing. Some books call them 'actors' because they do the action, but 'agent' is a more popular word.

If you have done Unit 5, you may remember how important it was to make sure that verbs and the number of people doing the verb were in agreement. In other words, the agents must agree with the verb used.

'They runs home' is non-standard English because 'they' is a plural word and 'runs' is a singular form of the verb.

'I likes teacakes' is non-standard English because 'I' is a first person singular pronoun and doesn't agree with 'likes' which is a third person singular form of the verb ('he likes' or 'she likes').

'We was very pleased' is non-standard because 'we' is a first person plural pronoun and doesn't agree with 'was' which is a third person singular form of the verb ('he was' and 'she was').

Leave **clauses** and **objects** aside for the time being, and just think about **agents** (or **subjects**) and **main verbs** for the moment.

Read the following story which is a well-known urban myth. An urban myth is a tale set in a modern town or city. Nobody knows who first told it, or even if it is true, yet it is amazing how it gets around. They are rather like jokes.

You may have heard this tale already in another version.

The Phantom Hitch Hiker

One autumn night a man and his daughter were driving home after an evening out. They had been to see a comedy film at the local cinema. They talked enthusiastically about it and laughed out loud whenever they remembered a particularly funny bit. Every so often, the man's daughter fed him a crisp from the packet she was finishing off.

The moon lit up the houses and the streets with a strange glow. The road was deserted and wet from the rain earlier in the evening. Suddenly, by the roadside, they saw a girl waving to them.

'I think she wants a lift,' said the man's daughter, as they drove past her.

Her father stopped the car just ahead of the hitch hiker who ran toward it. She was about seventeen, blonde and wore a denim suit. She carried a large bag over her shoulder.

'Oh thanks a lot. I'd be really grateful for a lift to my parents' house. It's just a mile or two up the road, right opposite the Green Dragon pub,' she said.

'Okay. Jump in,' said the man.

His daughter got out so that the girl could climb into the back seat.

'Off we go then,' said the man.

His daughter tried to chat to the hitch hiker but she did not seem to want to talk. She just stared out of the side window.

Soon they were approaching the Green Dragon. There was only one house directly opposite. You could see light shining through chinks in the curtains.

'Is this it?' asked the man. No reply came from the back of the car. His daughter turned round and was amazed to find that the girl wasn't there any more. She looked behind the seat. She peered into the darkness at the back of the car, but nowhere could she find the girl hitch hiker.

Her father got out, very puzzled and a little scared. There was no way that the girl could have got out of the car and yet she had disappeared completely.

'I'm going to have a word with her parents. I hope this is the right house.'

He knocked on the door. An elderly couple opened it very cautiously. The man

---

continued

apologised for disturbing them and explained what had happened. He also described the girl in detail.

The couple looked at each other and then at the man and his daughter.

'Yes. We do have a daughter just like the girl you saw. We haven't seen her since she ran away from home when she was fourteen. She was last seen hitch hiking one night along this very road three years ago. She has never been seen since. Today would have been her birthday.'

Now look at the first half of the story again with your Grammar Ray glasses. In the text that follows, all the agents have been circled and the main verbs underlined. Sometimes the agents and their main verbs are single words, sometimes they are chunks of words.

One autumn night (a man and his daughter) <u>were driving</u> home after an evening out. (They) <u>had been to see</u> a comedy film at the local cinema. (They) <u>talked</u> enthusiastically about it and <u>laughed</u> out loud whenever (they) <u>remembered</u> a particularly funny bit. Every so often, (the man's daughter) <u>fed</u> him a crisp from the packet (she) <u>was finishing off</u>.

(The moon) <u>lit up</u> the houses and the streets with a strange glow. (The road) <u>was</u> deserted and wet from the rain earlier in the evening. Suddenly, by the roadside, (they) <u>saw</u> a girl waving to them.

'(I) <u>think</u> (she) <u>wants</u> a lift,' <u>said</u> (the man's daughter,) as (they) <u>drove</u> past her.

(Her father) <u>stopped</u> the car just ahead of the (hitch hiker who) <u>ran</u> towards it. (She) <u>was</u> about seventeen, blonde and <u>wore</u> a denim suit. (She) <u>carried</u> a large bag over her shoulder.

'Oh thanks a lot. (I'd) <u>be</u> really grateful for a lift to my parents' house. (It's) just a mile or two up the road, right opposite the Green Dragon pub,' (she) <u>said</u>.

'Okay. Jump in,' <u>said</u> (the man.)

(His daughter) <u>got out</u> so that (the girl) <u>could climb</u> into the back seat.

'Off (we) <u>go</u> then,' <u>said</u> (her father.)

Notice the contractions: 'I'd' ('I would') and 'It's' ('It is').

You could summarise the story so far by just writing out the agents and their verbs:

a) A man and his daughter . . . were driving home.
b) They had been to see . . .
c) They talked . . . laughed . . . remembered . . .
d) . . . the man's daughter fed . . . she was finishing . . .
e) The moon lit up . . .
f) The road was . . .
g) . . . they saw . . .
h) Her father stopped . . . who (the hitch hiker) ran . . .
i) She was . . . wore

j) She carried . . .

k) I'd be . . .

l) It's . . .

m) . . . she said.

n) . . . Jump in,' said the man.

o) His daughter got out . . . the girl could climb . . .

p) . . . we go . . .,' said the man.

It isn't difficult to see all the agents and what they did, when written out this way. Now here are some questions for you to answer:

1 Where do agents (or subjects) most frequently appear in sentences? Are there any non-human subjects?

2 How many sentences have got more than one verb?

3 Does the main verb ever come before the agent?

4 Is there an example here of a main verb with a modal verb in front of it? (You may need to remind yourself about modal verbs.)

5 Explain why the pronoun 'who' has been used in sentence (h).

6 Often, the main verb comes straight after its agent, but sometimes it doesn't. Are there any sentences here in which the agents and the main verbs are separated by other words?

Now read the second half of the story and list the agents and the main verbs of each sentence. Set out your list like the one above, using dotted lines for the missing words.

So what are CLAUSES? Well, for one thing, they're not phrases.

> In these units the word **phrase** has been used from time to time. A phrase is a group of words (a chunk) as opposed to a single word.

Here are some phrases to remind you:

- fish and chips
- a great football manager
- a piece of cake
- Jack and Jill
- a sunny day
- the motor bike races
- a day in school
- a lovely birthday present

There are millions of them, and you could go on thinking them up from now until doomsday! But none of them will have a verb; there is nobody in a phrase doing anything, and no thing doing anything either. Even chunks of words like 'wearing a green coat' are phrases because they give you no exact idea of who is doing the wearing (the agent).

> Clauses are groups of words that do have an agent and at least one main verb in them.

The phrases on the previous page can easily be turned into clauses:

- I LIKE fish and chips.
- SHE IS a great football manager.
- I HAVE EATEN a piece of cake.
- JACK AND JILL WENT up the hill.
- IT WAS a sunny day.
- WE WENT to the motor bike races.
- HE MISSED a day in school.
- SHE RECEIVED a lovely birthday present.

In other words, a clause contains a subject and a main verb (you know who, or what, is doing what and when).

As people speak and write, they are thinking all the time in a mixture of phrases and clauses. In writing it is especially important to have sorted those thoughts out by the time they get to your pen or your keyboard.

The sentences you eventually write will consist of one clause or more than one clause.

> The examples above are all one-clause sentences. For that reason they are called **simple sentences**. A simple sentence is the same thing as a clause.

> If two of these clauses are fastened together by words like 'and', 'but' or 'then', you get two-clause sentences, called **compound sentences**.

Here are some compound sentences made from the simple sentences (or clauses) above:

- I like fish and chips and I have eaten a piece of cake.
- It was a sunny day and Jack and Jill went up the hill.
- We went to the motor bike races and we missed a day in school.

They are not the world's greatest sentences, but you should be able to see the point.

> The clauses used in all the examples so far are called **main** or **independent clauses**. This means that they can stand on their own as sentences, beginning with a capital letter and ending with a full stop.

There is one other kind of clause that is called a **subordinate** or **dependent clause**. These almost always begin with one of those connectors (conjunctions) you looked at in Unit Eight (for example, if, when, whenever, although, until, because, though, where, wherever, therefore, despite). The best clue to a subordinate (or dependent) clause is usually the first word in the clause. 'Subordinate' and 'dependent' mean the same thing. Use the name you prefer.

Subordinate clauses depend upon a main clause that can stand as a sentence by itself.

Here are some main clauses:

- You can go out this weekend.
- You cannot watch television.
- Your ideas are good.
- You are the only person here.
- You can play your computer game.

Now look at the difference the addition of a subordinate clause can make:

- You can go out this weekend, if you get your jobs done.
- You cannot watch television, until you have done your homework.
- Your ideas are good, although your handwriting is atrocious.
- You must have done it, because you were the only person there.
- You can play your computer game, when you have washed up.

You've heard them all before no doubt!

They can even be written back to front:

- If you get your jobs done, you can go out this weekend.
- Until you have done your homework, you cannot watch television.
- Although your handwriting is atrocious, your ideas are good.
- Because you were the only person there, you must have done it.
- When you have washed up, you can play your computer game.

The main (independent) clauses can stand alone as sentences, the subordinate clauses cannot, because they are incomplete. It is the underlined word that tells you that there is another bit to the sentence.

- <u>If</u> you get your jobs done . . .
- <u>Until</u> you have done your homework . . .
- <u>Although</u> your handwriting is atrocious . . .
- <u>Because</u> you were the only person there . . .
- <u>When</u> you have washed up . . .

> Sentences with two or more main (or independent) clauses in them are called **compound sentences**. (For example, 'I've had some fish and chips and I've eaten an ice cream and I've drunk three cokes and I've been on the big dipper and I think I'm going to be sick.')

> Sentences with one or more subordinate (or dependent clauses) are called **complex sentences**. That doesn't mean they are any more complicated; it just means they have one or more dependents to support!

The key to clauses is the fact that they contain an agent (subject) and a main verb. So what are OBJECTS?

Look back at *The Phantom Hitch Hiker* and find the following:

a) They had been to see a comedy film at the local cinema.
b) . . . the man's daughter fed him a crisp . . .
c) The moon lit up the houses and the streets . . .
d) Her father stopped the car . . .
e) She carried a large bag . . .

Texts are full of subjects (agents) and main verbs, but they also contain lots of objects.

> Objects in grammar are persons or things that are not doing the main action but are very often having it done to them or near them.

> There are two kinds of objects: **direct objects** and **indirect objects**.

In the five examples above, the objects are:

DIRECT	INDIRECT
A comedy film A crisp The houses and the streets The car A large bag	the local cinema (to) him

Can you work out what the difference is from these examples? Put the difference in your own words first. Write it down. Then compare your idea with the description that follows.

> When the verb acts directly on the object as in: to see a comedy film; offered a crisp; lit up the houses; stopped the car, the object is said to be a **direct object**.
>
> When it does not act directly on the object but acts in relation to it, the object is said to be **indirect**. Usually a preposition gives you the clue, as in: AT the local cinema.
>
> Good examples to help you remember the difference are the following:
>
> The dog ate the bone ('bone' is a direct object).
> The cat sat on the mat ('mat' is an indirect object).
>
> BUT (in nonsense land):
>
> The dog ate the mat (now 'mat' has become a direct object).
> The cat sat on the bone (now 'bone' has become an indirect object).
>
> AND THE CONSEQUENCE WAS:
>
> The dog ate the cat!! (now the poor cat has become a direct object!!).

One thing to look out for is the indirect object that doesn't have a preposition like 'on' in 'on the mat'.

Look at the following example:

> The teacher gave the girl a book.

Explain why 'book' is the direct object and 'girl' is the indirect object. What is the missing preposition?

Compare this example with one from *The Phantom Hitch Hiker*:

> . . . the man's daughter offered him a crisp . . .

Which is the direct object here ('him'? or 'a crisp'?) and which is the indirect object? What was actually being given or offered, 'him' or 'a crisp'?

Finally, here are some activities to practise your knowledge of agents, objects, clauses and subordinating conjunctions. What a mouthful! But it isn't anything like as difficult as rocket science!

1 Here is a list of noun phrases:

a) a great pop group
b) her new dress
c) purple people eaters
d) rotten apples
e) Venusian cyberwomen

In sentences these noun phrases could be either agents or objects. Write two sentences for each phrase, making it an agent in one and an object in the other. Your objects can be direct or indirect. Don't forget to punctuate properly.

2 Look at the following subordinating conjunctions (connectors). Write two clauses that would go with them. Watch out for the connectors that come at the very beginning.

a) …………despite…………
b) If…………………………
c) ……………although……
d) Because…………………..
e) …………when…………..

3 Choose a paragraph of at least three sentences from any text in Units 1 to 15 and do a grammatical analysis of the agents, the main verbs and any clause connectors. Remember that the clause connectors might be simple ones like 'and' or complex ones like 'I', 'when', 'because' etc.
Put a circle round the agents (subjects); underline any main verbs; and put square brackets round a clause connecting word.
Here is an example from the text on dinosaurs in Unit Four:

[If] you stop to think about it, the fascination with dinosaurs is all a bit strange. Look at it this way: have you ever seen a real live dinosaur from long ago? Nope, neither have we. All we've ever seen have been reconstructions made by scientists – collections of bones, wired together to make a skeleton, or life size model built of plaster and resin.

Notice that when command verbs have been used, the agent (subject) 'you' is often implied, as in '(You) Look at it this way . . .'. Notice also that in questions the agent and main verb are reversed, as in '. . . have you ever seen . . ?'. Most of the time you would expect to put a circle then an underline. Occasionally you have to underline the verb first, then circle the agent, as in, 'Nope, neither have we'.

Always watch out for contractions like 'we've . . . seen' which means 'we have . . . seen' (agent + verb).

This last unit is called A Last Word on Sentences but you will have noticed that much of it has been about verbs. This is as it should be, because verbs are the key element in clauses and sentences.

In Unit Twelve you investigated an important difference in the way that verbs can be used: they may be used in the active or the passive. These two different ways have traditionally been called the active and the passive voice. As the final part of this unit you are going to look at another important difference in the use of verbs, and the difference has traditionally been described by the terms TRANSITIVE and INTRANSITIVE VERBS.

141

> Transitive verbs take direct objects (see p139) while intransitive verbs don't.

Here are some examples. First, transitive verbs with their direct objects. The verbs have been underlined, the direct objects circled:

a) They <u>beat</u> (the carpet) all afternoon.

b) They <u>shot</u> (ten rounds) of ammunition.

c) She <u>picked</u> (some flowers.)

d) The doctor <u>cured</u> (his patient.)

e) I shall <u>open</u> (the door) when I am ready.

f) <u>Ring</u> (the bell) please.

g) I'm forever <u>blowing</u> (bubbles.)

Now for some intransitive verbs. The verbs have been underlined:

a) The volcano <u>erupted</u>.

b) Torrential rain <u>fell</u>.

c) The sun <u>rose</u>.

d) Uncle Jim and Auntie Flo <u>came</u>.

e) It <u>will happen</u>.

f) They <u>waited</u>.

g) The girl <u>blushed</u>.

Can you see that the action of transitive verbs 'passes over' to an object? Transitive means just that, 'passing over'.
Intransitive verbs do not pass over to anything at all. They just ARE! You can put an adverb after the intransitive verbs, but not a noun.

1 Write out the seven sentences with intransitive verbs and add an adverb to them. The adverb can tell when, where or how the verb took place, for example 'Torrential rain fell for a whole month' (the adverb phrase tells you how long).

2 Think of three transitive verbs and write a sentence for each of them.

3 Think of three intransitive verbs (it may help to scan a dictionary) and put them in sentences ending with an adverb or an adverbial phrase.

4 Because the English language is extraordinarily flexible in the way it is used, some verbs can be used both transitively and intransitively. Here are some examples of such verbs:

read,   play,   explode,   blush,   enjoy,   sing,   choke.

Write two sentences for each verb, one using it transitively, the other using it intransitively. You can put the verb in any tense you like.

Glossary

Abstract noun – a noun that is more like an idea or a feeling, rather than a thing, e.g. success, happiness.

Acronym – a word made out of the initial letters of other words, e.g. Disc Jockey = DJ = deejay.

Adjective – a word that describes a noun, e.g. a large loaf; a good game; a fast runner. The comparative form uses 'more' or adds 'er', as in 'more helpful' and 'faster'. The superlative form uses 'most' or adds 'est', as in 'most helpful' and 'fastest'.

Adverb (adverbial) – a word or phrase that tells you when, where and how the verb was done, e.g. he walked last night; he walked in the garden; he walked quickly.

Agent – the person (or thing) who does the action of the verb, e.g. the man laughed; the car crashed.

Alliteration – repeated use of an initial consonant, e.g. 'Tiny tots try terrible tantrums at teatime'.

Ambiguity – when a word or phrase has two or more meanings it is said to be ambiguous, e.g. 'Go and ask the butcher if he has got any brains'.

Antonym – an opposite meaning, e.g. sad/happy; fast/slow; large/small.

Apostrophe – usually indicates a missing letter, e.g. 'doesn't it' or possession, e.g. 'John's football boots'.

Article – 'the' is the definite article; 'a' and 'an' are the indefinite articles.

Assonance – a repeated vowel sound, e.g. 'The rain in Spain falls mainly on the plain'.

Auxiliary verbs – usually a form of the verb 'to be' and the verb 'to have'; they help other verbs.

Command – one of the four sentence functions.

Connectives (connectors) – words that connect or fasten other words (see conjunctions and prepositions).

Clause – a group of words containing a subject and a main verb.

Concrete noun – one you can see, hear, smell, touch, taste; all the things in the physical world.

Consonant – the twenty-one letters of the alphabet that aren't 'a,e,i,o,u', but remember that there are 24 consonants in English speech.

Declarative – same thing as a statement.

Demonstrative pronoun – 'this' and 'that'.

Derivation – a word derived from another word, e.g. nation/nationality; accept/acceptance; home/homely.

Digraph – two letters together, e.g. some vowel digraphs are: 'ie', 'ea', 'ou'.

Direct speech – speech as it happens, usually put between inverted commas (speech marks) in writing.

Etymology – the study of the origins and development of words and their meanings.

Exclamation – ah! Ooh! I say! Great! Rubbish! Heck!

Explicit – expressing details in a clear and obvious way. The popular phrase 'spelling it out' means the same thing. The opposite is implicit meaning, see *implication* below.

Finite verb – with a finite verb you definitely know who (or what) did the action and when, e.g. in the phrase 'grinning sheepishly' you have no idea at all who is grinning; in the clause 'They grinned sheepishly' you know who grinned and that it was in the past.

Gerund – the present participle of a verb used as a noun, e.g. A book on Hiking; smoking is bad for you.

Grammatical words – all the little words that hold everything together but don't have any meaning in themselves; they do essential jobs, e.g. prepositions, conjunctions and the auxiliaries.

Homographs – words that look alike but which are pronounced differently, e.g. wind up the clock; blowin' in the wind.

Homonyms – words that look exactly alike but have different meanings, e.g. an 'ear' for listening with and an 'ear' of corn; 'I can't bear bears'.

Homophones – words that sound alike but have different spellings and meanings, e.g. they rode along the road.

Impersonal pronoun – it.

Imperative – a command, verb or sentence.

Implication/imply – writers and speakers can imply or hint at meanings rather than state them explicitly; don't confuse these words with *infer* and *inference* (see below).

Indirect speech – speech that is reported by somebody else, usually introduced or followed by 'he said' or an equivalent.

Inference/infer – readers and listeners infer (guess at or deduce) meanings implied by writers and speakers.

Infinitive – a form of the verb that always begins with the word 'to', e.g. 'to go', 'to sing', 'to fly'.

Intensifier – an adverb that intensifies (makes stronger) the meaning of an adjective or another adverb, e.g. very enjoyable; really, really good; she ran very quickly.

Interrogative – a question word like What? Who? Why?

Intonation – the ups and downs and the 'tunes' of speech that carry so much meaning and often tell you where someone comes from.

Intransitive verb – a verb that doesn't take an object, e.g. I slept; I cried; I laughed; I blushed; I walked. These all make sense in their own right; you can put a full stop after them. Now look up *transitive verb* (below) to find out the difference.

Irregular verb – one of two classes of English verbs (the other class is regular, see below); they are irregular because their tense endings do not follow a regular pattern, e.g. buy/bought (not 'buyed'); go/went (not 'goed'); think/thought (not 'thinked').

Lexical word – all the nouns, adjectives, verbs and adverbs are lexical words because they contain meanings; they are distinct from *grammatical words* (see above).

Metaphor – the use of a word to make a meaning that is understandable but not literally so, e.g. He cried buckets; her eyes swept the room; I'm over the moon.

Noun – the name of a person, place or thing; it can be proper, common, concrete, abstract, singular, plural and part of a noun phrase.

Object – something the verb acts on directly or indirectly, e.g. The boy kicked the ball ('ball' is a direct object); The boy fell in the water ('the water' is an indirect object).

Onomatopoeia – the way some words sound like the sound they represent, e.g. splash, crack, bang.

Past participle – the part of the verb that indicates past tense, e.g. boiled, spent, broken, taught. They make very good adjectives, e.g. boiled sweets, spent cartridge, broken promises, self-taught guitarist.

Personal pronouns – I, he, she, they, we, you.

Phoneme – for example, one of the 44 sounds that make up spoken English (24 spoken consonants and 20 vowel sounds).

Phonology – the sound system (phonemes) of a language.

Phrase – two or more words that convey meaning but don't contain a main verb.

Possessive pronouns – my, your, our, their, his, her, its.

Preposition – a word that positions, or locates, nouns e.g. under the bed; in the kitchen; behind the fridge.

Present participle – that part of the verb that indicates present tense, e.g. running, laughing, fishing. They are very good for making adjectives with, e.g. running shoes; laughing gas; fishing tackle (see also *gerund*).

Pronoun – a word that stands for a noun (see also under *personal, reflexive, possessive, demonstrative, relative* and *impersonal pronouns*).

Question – one of the four sentence functions (the others are *statement, command, exclamation*).

Qualifier – a word, usually an adverb, used to qualify something you want to say, e.g. slightly difficult; rather awkward; mostly enjoyable; less helpful.

Reflexive pronoun – myself, herself, himself, yourself, themselves, yourselves, ourselves.

Regular verb – a verb that conjugates in a regular fashion, i.e. there is no radical change in the middle of the word (as in irregular verbs), e.g. I walk/she walks; I walked/she walked.

Relative pronoun – who, whom, whose, which, that.

Rhythm – the dah-de-dah-de-dah-de-dah of speech and poetry; they vary a great deal.

Simile – a way of comparing, usually by saying something is 'like' or 'as' something else, e.g. as free as air; he fell like a stone; she ran like mad; I'm as happy as a lark.

Statement – one of the four sentence functions; sometimes called 'declaratives'; they state or declare something to be so.

Stress – laying emphasis on a syllable or a whole word, especially in speech, to make a meaning stronger.

Subordinating conjunction – a connecting word like 'although', 'because', 'if' and 'when', that does more than coordinating conjunctions such as 'and' or 'then'.

Subject – the person or thing that a clause or sentence is saying something about.

Syntax – the joining up of words into phrases, clauses and sentences to make meanings; word order.

Syllable – a part of the sound pattern of a word; a vowel is a key element of a syllable.

Transitive verb – a verb that takes a direct object, e.g. she ate the cakes; he painted the door; they lifted the box; she gave a pen to her brother; we opened a savings account; you take the heavy bag.

Verb – yes, a doing word is still as good a description as any, so long as you include 'being', 'having', 'seeming' and a few others.

Verbatim – speech as it was spoken; direct speech; a kind of reporting.

Vowel – the famous five of the English alphabet (a, e, i, o, u), along with 'y' now and again; there are 20 vowel phonemes in English which accounts for some spelling headaches.